108課網
贏戰統測

20分鐘
稱霸統測
英文
綜合測驗

隨書附贈解析本

莊靜軒、蕭美玲　編著

- 面對分秒必爭的考生生活，你該如何分配時間？
- 面對各式各樣的考試內容，你該如何抓住重點？
每天 20 分鐘，快速練習統測英文綜合測驗

東大圖書公司

國家圖書館出版品預行編目資料

20分鐘稱霸統測英文綜合測驗／莊靜軒,蕭美玲編著.
——初版四刷.——臺北市: 東大，2022
　　面；　公分

　　ISBN 978-957-19-3149-4 （平裝）
　1. 英語教育 2. 中等教育

524.38　　　　　　　　　　　　　106021583

贏 戰統測

20 分鐘稱霸統測英文綜合測驗

編 著 者	莊靜軒　蕭美玲
企劃編輯	陳逸如
責任編輯	劉倩茹
美術編輯	黃顯喬

發 行 人	劉仲傑
出 版 者	東大圖書股份有限公司
地　　址	臺北市復興北路 386 號 (復北門市)
	臺北市重慶南路一段 61 號 (重南門市)
電　　話	(02)25006600
網　　址	三民網路書店 https://www.sanmin.com.tw

出版日期	初版一刷 2018 年 1 月
	初版四刷 2022 年 2 月
書籍編號	E804570
I S B N	978-957-19-3149-4

東大圖書公司

序

在面對分秒必爭的考生生活，你該如何分配時間？
在面對各式各樣的考試內容，你該如何抓住重點？

每天 20 分鐘，快速練習統測英文綜合測驗。

　　本書參考測驗中心近年公布的歷屆試題撰寫，期望讀者能運用每天 20 分鐘的時間，輕鬆完成測驗題型之練習。綜合測驗的特色在於考生需要具備更加完整的應考能力，同時兼顧各類字詞用法及文法觀念。因此特別針對綜合測驗，製作本書讓讀者加強練習，以增強其在考試時的得分能力。

　　本書共 12 個單元，每單元的綜合測驗題皆包含兩篇短文。全書文章內容多元，並整理出 48 個統測重要句型及 240 個常見單字，讓讀者能在 20 分鐘完成兩篇綜合測驗練習題之後，有條理地學習文章內所運用到的單字及文法句型。另外，隨書附贈活動式解析夾冊，內容包含完整的文章中文翻譯以及詳盡的試題解析，讓讀者在做完練習題之後，能夠立即檢視自己的學習成效。

　　希望藉由本書讓讀者能循序漸進的練習與學習，最終稱霸統測英文綜合測驗。本書雖再三校閱，但仍恐有疏漏之處，敬請各界先進與讀者海涵與不吝賜教。

Step 1

每天運用 20 分鐘，完成兩篇綜合測驗（Part 1+Part 2），每篇文章皆包含五題單選題。

〉小叮嚀〈

答案的部分請翻閱解析夾冊。

Step 2

在練習完題目之後，再利用「字彙補給站」及「文法加油站」的內容，學習文章內所提及的單字及文法。每篇文章，皆有一個「字彙補給站」及一個「文法加油站」，按照文章排序分為 Part 1 兩頁及 Part 2 兩頁。

Step 3

活動式解析夾冊的設計，讓讀者輕鬆對照文章及題目，其內容包含文章中譯及詳盡的題目解析。

〉小叮嚀〈

在解析裡看到 ➕ 文法加油站 1 時，可以翻至當回次的「文法加油站」，看更詳細的文法解釋及補充例句喔！

20分鐘 稱霸統測 英文綜合測驗　Unit 1

Part 1
The History of the Elevator

The history of the elevator can be traced back all the way to Roman times when slaves pulled ropes to raise and lower platforms up and down between floors. It was not until 1823 __1__ the first steam-powered elevators were invented. Two British architects developed a steam-powered "ascending room" taking tourists up to a high platform __2__ they could enjoy a view of London. Newer designs allowed bigger and better elevators to be used in buildings. __3__ , there was a major disadvantage: the elevators were terribly unsafe. Thankfully, in 1852, Elisha Otis invented a new type of elevator to __4__ the safety problem. The key feature of the Otis elevator is its safety device which prevents the elevator __5__ falling. Today, the Otis Elevator Company is still one the largest elevator manufacturers in the world with its elevators installed in some famous structures like the Eiffel Tower, Japan's first skyscraper, and so on.

1. (A) who (B) that (C) which (D) where
2. (A) where (B) when (C) which (D) why
3. (A) Therefore (B) Surprisingly (C) However (D) Furthermore
4. (A) hide (B) solve (C) support (D) interrupt
5. (A) in (B) for (C) with (D) from

Part 2
Let's Go to the Toy Hall of Fame

Toys have been a part of human culture throughout the recorded history. __1__ many of our modern toys would be unrecognizable to children from years past, some toys have remained popular over the centuries. The Toy Hall of Fame is located in New York. It is a museum __2__ collects the greatest classic toys from past and present. It includes __3__ toys such as bubbles, kites, balls and playing cards. Besides, it also consists of everyday __4__ that are not normally considered to be toys, like cardboard boxes, blankets and sticks. Children here seem to be able to create a toy or game out of anything. __5__ a little imagination, hours of fun can be had with any object that happens to be nearby at the time. The museum is really worth visiting, so don't miss it if you take a trip to New York.

1. (A) If (B) While (C) Because (D) As long as
2. (A) where (B) whom (C) whose (D) which
3. (A) familiar (B) domestic (C) temporary (D) commercial
4. (A) sources (B) images (C) objects (D) prizes
5. (A) In (B) Of (C) For (D) With

字彙補給站　Part 1

1. elevator (n.) 電梯
   We couldn't take the elevator to the top floor because it was under repaired.
2. trace back 追溯至
   In order to know more about her family's history, the woman traced it back to the nineteenth century.
3. slave (n.) 奴隸
   The slave trade during the sixteenth century was cruel.
4. architect (n.) 建築師
   A professional architect should be cautious about his / her design and construction of the building for the sake of public safety.
5. disadvantage (n.) 缺點，壞處
   One of the disadvantages of exposing to too much sun is getting tanned.

文法加油站

1

It be 被強調的部分 that...

說明：

此句型表示「就是…；正是…」，用來加強語氣使用，目的是強調句中的某個部分。被強調的部分若是擬入，則 that 可以替換成 who。強調的部分可以是原句子中的主詞、受詞、時間副詞、地方副詞或副詞子句等等，但不強調動詞。例如文中：It was not until 1823 that the first steam-powered elevators were invented. (強調時間)。

* 原句：I met John in the supermarket last night.
* 強調句：It was in the supermarket that I met John last night. (強調地點)
   It was last night that I met John in the supermarket. (強調時間)
   It was John that / who I met in the supermarket last night. (強調人)

字彙補給站　Part 2

1. culture (n.) 文化
   The culture of racial minorities is facing an increasingly dying situation.
2. throughout (prep.) 遍及；遍布
   The rumor spread throughout the whole country.
3. unrecognizable (adj.) 無法辨識的
   Some of the sentences on this page were unrecognizable, so I couldn't get a whole idea of the passage.
4. collect (v.) 收集；蒐羅
   In Meg's painting, colorful flowers were used to collect the coming of spring.
5. include (v.) 包含，包括
   All important information about the party was included in the invitation card. You could take a look at it.
6. normally (adv.) 一般地；通常
   The first bus normally arrives at the nearest stop around 6:30 a.m.
7. be able to 能夠
   We are not pretty sure whether Jessica will be able to come to the party or not.
8. imagination (n.) 想像力
   With his vivid imagination, Joe became one of the best-selling authors.
9. happen (v.) 碰巧
   Louis happened to meet William at the train station last Sunday.
10. nearby (adv.) 在附近
   Is there any Italian restaurant nearby?

文法加油站

1

With + N, S + V...

說明：

此句型表示「有…的狀態」、「由於有…」或「透過…；藉由…」等。以 with + N 引導一種情境或是表示一種原因，引導或附帶說明主要句子的語意。例如文中：With a little imagination, hours of fun can be had...。

* With this one-day pass, you can visit as many places in the city as you can.
* With some tricks, the clown amazed the children and made them laugh loudly.

2

S + be worth + N / V-ing / 數字 (金額)

說明：

此句型表示「值得…；值得…」，其中的 worth 為形容詞，之後常加上名詞、V-ing、數字 (金額)，例如文中：The museum is really worth visiting, so...。

* Kenting National Park is worth visiting. = Kenting National Park is worth a visit.
* The watch my husband gave me is worth over 10,000 dollars.

Unit 1

Part 1 The History of the Elevator

中譯：

電梯的由來可以一直回溯至羅馬時代，奴隸拉繩讓平台在樓層間升降。直到 1823 年第一座蒸氣驅動的電梯才問世。兩位英國建築師發明蒸氣驅動的「升降室」帶觀光客到能欣賞美景的高台。較佳的設計讓大樓裡的電梯變得更大更好。然而，卻有一個重大缺點：非常不安全。所幸，1852 年，伊萊莎·奧的斯發明一種新型電梯來解決安全問題。奧的斯電梯的關鍵特色是防電梯墜落的安全裝置。時至今日，奧的斯電梯公司仍舊是全球最大電梯製造商之一，連艾菲爾鐵塔和日本首座摩天大樓等知名建築，都裝有奧的斯的電梯。

解析：

1. 此句型為 It be 被強調的部分 that...，目的是強調句中的某部分，強調的部分不可為動詞，此句強調詞為「not until 1823」。➔ 文法加油站 1
2. 此處應先行詞為 platform，在形容詞子句中是一地點，故答案選 (A) 關係副詞 where。若將關係副詞 which 改插，須將介係詞 on 併回，例句中：a high platform where they could enjoy a view of London = a high platform on which they could enjoy a view of London.
3. 前述在說明電梯經改良的情況，而後述點出缺點，故以此轉折值氣，故答案選 (C) However 然而。(A) Therefore 因此 (B) Surprisingly 意外地 (C) Furthermore 此外，再不列讀意。
4. (A) hide (v.) 躲藏 (B) solve (v.) 解決 (C) support (v.) 支持 (D) interrupt (v.) 中斷。
5. 此處意為「防電梯墜落…」而 prevent / keep / stop...from + N / V-ing 表示預防 / 避免 / 阻止…做…，所以選 (D) from。➔ 文法加油站 1

Part 2 Let's Go to the Toy Hall of Fame

中譯：

玩具一直是人類文化的一部分。雖然許多現代玩具已經很難讓過去的孩子認出來，但也有一些玩具，歷經世紀永久風行不墜。玩具名人堂座落於紐約。那是個搜集古往今來經典玩具的博物館。其中包括例如氣泡、風箏、球和紙牌。此外，它有一般不會被視為玩具的日常物品，像是厚紙板、毯子和木棍。小孩子在這似乎不管拿到任何東西，都能變做玩具及發明玩具。只要一點想像力，身邊的任何東西都能帶來數小時的樂趣。這座博物館實值得造訪，所以如果你到紐約旅行，別錯過了。

解析：

1. 此題順意為「雖然許多現代玩具已經很難讓過去的孩子認出來…」所以根據語意，本題選 (B) While 雖然，儘管。
2. 此題句關係子句的概念，先行詞為 museum，關係代名詞是主格，故選 (D) which。
3. 從 bubbles, kites, balls and playing cards 可知道些都是常見的玩具，故根據前後語意 (A) familiar (adj.) 熟悉的，其餘選項均不符合語意。(B) domestic (adj.) 國內的，本國的 (C) temporary (adj.) 暫時的 (D) commercial (adj.) 商業的。
4. 從 cardboard boxes, blankets and sticks 可知道些都是常見的物品，故本題選 (C) objects 物品。
5. 此題順意為「只要一點想像力，身邊的任何東西都能帶來數小時的樂趣。」，故答案選 (D) With 有…的情況下。with + N 的句型，是用來引導一種情境或是表示一種原因，附帶說明主要句子的語意。➔ 文法加油站 1

Acknowledgements: The articles in this publication are
adapted from the works by: Peter Wilds and Barbara Cromarty.
Photo credit: depositphotos.

▶ **Part 1**

The History of the Elevator

The history of the elevator can be traced back all the way to Roman times when slaves pulled ropes to raise and lower platforms up and down between floors. It was not until 1823 __1__ the first steam-powered elevators were invented. Two British architects developed a steam-powered "ascending room" taking tourists up to a high platform __2__ they could enjoy a view of London. Newer designs allowed bigger and better elevators to be used in buildings. __3__, there was a major disadvantage: the elevators were terribly unsafe. Thankfully, in 1852, Elisha Otis invented a new type of elevator to __4__ the safety problem. The key feature of the Otis elevator is its safety device which prevents the elevator __5__ falling. Today, the Otis Elevator Company is still one of the largest elevator manufacturers in the world with its elevators installed in some famous structures like the Eiffel Tower, Japan's first skyscraper, and so on.

_____ 1. (A) who   (B) that   (C) which   (D) where

_____ 2. (A) where   (B) when   (C) which   (D) why

_____ 3. (A) Therefore   (B) Surprisingly   (C) However   (D) Furthermore

_____ 4. (A) hide   (B) solve   (C) support   (D) interrupt

_____ 5. (A) in   (B) for   (C) with   (D) from

▶ *Part 2*

Let's Go to the Toy Hall of Fame

Toys have been a part of human culture throughout the recorded history. __1__ many of our modern toys would be unrecognizable to children from years past, some toys have remained popular over the centuries. The Toy Hall of Fame is located in New York. It is a museum __2__ collects the greatest classic toys from past and present. It includes __3__ toys such as bubbles, kites, balls and playing cards. Besides, it also consists of everyday __4__ that are not normally considered to be toys, like cardboard boxes, blankets and sticks. Children here seem to be able to create a toy or game out of anything. __5__ a little imagination, hours of fun can be had with any object that happens to be nearby at the time. The museum is really worth visiting, so don't miss it if you take a trip to New York.

_____ 1. (A) If   (B) While   (C) Because   (D) As long as

_____ 2. (A) where   (B) whom   (C) whose   (D) which

_____ 3. (A) familiar   (B) domestic   (C) temporary   (D) commercial

_____ 4. (A) sources   (B) images   (C) objects   (D) prizes

_____ 5. (A) In   (B) Of   (C) For   (D) With

➕ 字彙補給站

1. **elevator** (*n.*) 電梯

   We couldn't take the elevator to the top floor because it was under repair.

2. **trace back** 追溯至

   In order to know more about her family's history, the woman traced it back to the nineteenth century.

3. **slave** (*n.*) 奴隸

   The slave trade during the sixteenth century was cruel.

4. **architect** (*n.*) 建築師

   A professional architect should be cautious about his / her design and construction of the building for the sake of public safety.

5. **disadvantage** (*n.*) 缺點，壞處

   One of the disadvantages of being exposed to too much sun is getting tanned.

6. **terribly** (*adv.*) 很，非常

   Gary felt terribly upset when he flunked his math exam again.

7. **feature** (*n.*) 特色；特徵

   The main feature of the new cell phone is its lasting power.

8. **manufacturer** (*n.*) 製造商，生產商

   The company is the largest computer manufacturer in the world.

9. **install** (*v.*) 安裝

   My parents are going to call the plumber to come to install the new air conditioner.

10. **structure** (*n.*) 建築物

    The historic wooden structure was badly damaged in the fire.

✚ 文法加油站

It be 被強調的部分 that...

說明：

　　此句型表示「就是…；正是…」，用來加強語氣使用，目的是強調句中的某個部分。被強調的部分若是指人，則 that 可以替換成 who。強調的部分可以是原句子中的主詞、受詞、時間副詞、地方副詞或副詞子句等等，但不強調動詞。例如文中：It was not until 1823 that the first steam-powered elevators were invented. (強調時間)。

★ 原句：I met John in the supermarket last night.

★ 強調句：It was in the supermarket that I met John last night. (強調地點)

　　　　　It was last night that I met John in the supermarket. (強調時間)

　　　　　It was John that / who I met in the supermarket last night. (強調人)

S (+ Aux) + be + Vpp

說明：

　　此句型為被動語態，其重點在「承受」某動作的人或物上。主詞為承受動作的人或物。例如文中：Newer designs allowed bigger and better elevators to be used in buildings.。

★ The road is being repaired and we need to change our route to the station.

★ The report must be finished before tomorrow, so I have to stay up tonight.

➕ 字彙補給站

1. **culture** (*n.*) 文化

   The culture of racial minorities is facing an increasingly dying situation.

2. **throughout** (*prep.*) 遍及;遍布

   The rumor spread throughout the whole country.

3. **unrecognizable** (*adj.*) 無法辨識的

   Some of the sentences on this page were unrecognizable, so I couldn't get a whole idea of the passage.

4. **collect** (*v.*) 收集;聚積

   David has collected various stamps for years.

5. **include** (*v.*) 包含,包括

   All important information about the party was included in the invitation card. You could take a look at it.

6. **normally** (*adv.*) 一般地;通常

   The first bus normally arrives at the nearest stop around 6:30 a.m.

7. **be able to** 能夠

   We are not pretty sure whether Jessica will be able to come to the party or not.

8. **imagination** (*n.*) 想像力

   With his vivid imagination, Joe became one of the best-selling authors.

9. **happen** (*v.*) 碰巧

   Louis happened to meet William at the train station last Sunday.

10. **nearby** (*adv.*) 在附近

    Is there any Italian restaurant nearby?

➕ 文法加油站

With + N, S + V...

說明 ：

　　此句型表示「有…的狀態」、「由於有…」或「透過…；藉由…」等。
以 with + N，引導一種情境或表示一種原因，引導或附帶說明主要句子的語意。例如文中：With a little imagination, hours of fun can be had...。

★ With this one-day pass, you can visit as many places in the city as you can.

★ With some tricks, the clown amazed the children and made them laugh loudly.

2
S + be worth + N / V-ing / 數字 (金額)

說明 ：

　　此句型表示「值得…；價值…」，其中的 worth 為形容詞，之後需加上名詞、
V-ing、數字 (金額)，例如文中：The museum is really worth visiting, so...。

★ Kenting National Park is worth visiting. = Kenting National Park is worth a visit.

★ The watch my husband gave me is worth over 10,000 dollars.

▶ *Part 1*

It's Time to Start Eating Bugs Again

It is said that modern humans left Africa roughly 125,000 years ago and gradually spread across the entire globe. The places where people live range from tropical rainforests __1__ crowded cities. Thus, __2__ was not surprising that humans could survive on a wide variety of food. Nowadays, the __3__ diet is limited to a few crops, such as wheat, corn, and rice, and a handful of farm animals, like cows, pigs, and chickens. However, humans __4__ consume pretty much anything and that included insects. Insects are a great source of protein. Besides, raising insects for food has little negative impact __5__ the environment. Many people believe we should all start eating bugs again, for the sake of our health and for the planet.

_____ 1. (A) with   (B) to   (C) into   (D) for

_____ 2. (A) it   (B) this   (C) a person   (D) that

_____ 3. (A) positive   (B) modern   (C) complete   (D) meaningful

_____ 4. (A) used to   (B) are used to   (C) were used to   (D) being used to

_____ 5. (A) in   (B) for   (C) as   (D) on

▶ *Part 2*

Say "No" to Bottled Water

Health experts often suggest that people drink enough water during the day, especially when the weather is hot. Because of the convenience, there is a huge demand __1__ bottled water. It is estimated that every year consumers around the world __2__ over US$ 100 billion on bottled water. __3__ it is cheap and convenient to drink bottled water, there is a huge environmental cost because plastic bottles are made from oil and chemicals. __4__, a lot of fuel must be burned to send bottles of water to thirsty customers around the globe. So the next time you buy a bottle of water, __5__ the negative effect it has on our planet. Try to bring your own bottle and be friendly to our environment!

_____1. (A) of   (B) to   (C) at   (D) for

_____2. (A) cost   (B) take   (C) spend   (D) pay

_____3. (A) Since   (B) Though   (C) Before   (D) When

_____4. (A) Luckily   (B) However   (C) In addition   (D) As a result

_____5. (A) think about   (B) thought about (C) thinking about (D) to think about

➕ 字彙補給站

1. **roughly** (*adv.*) 大約，差不多

   Roughly estimated, there were about one thousand people joining the <u>demonstration</u> (示威；遊行) this morning.

2. **gradually** (*adv.*) 逐漸地

   With the medical care of his doctor, the man's health is gradually improving.

3. **range** (*v.*) 範圍涵蓋…

   The areas ranging from Taichung City to Nantou County were influenced by a power outage.

4. **survive** (*v.*) 存活；倖存

   It was a grief that no one survived in the tour bus crash.

5. **limit** (*v.*) 限制

   The organizers asked the competitors to limit their speech to five minutes maximum.

6. **such as** 例如；像是

   Amy brought a lot of fruit such as pineapples and grapes to the party.

7. **consume** (*v.*) 消費；消耗；飲用；食用

   Milk is recommended to be consumed within 10 days.

8. **protein** (*n.*) 蛋白質

   Beans and nuts are the main sources of protein for vegetarians.

9. **impact** (*n.*) 影響

   The new policy has made a great impact on the society.

10. **for the sake of** 因為；為了…

    Rita worked day and night for the sake of supporting her family.

➕ 文法加油站

S used to + V 曾經…

S be used to + N / V-ing 習慣於…

S be used to + V 被用來…

說明

　　此三個句型根據語意不同，其後所接的動詞型式也有所不同，例如文中：humans <u>used to consume</u> pretty much anything and that included insects. ，表示過去人們食用食物的情形。

★ William <u>used to be</u> my boyfriend. (表曾經的情況或過去常做的動作)

★ Nancy <u>is used to drinking</u> a cup of hot tea after taking a bath. (表示習慣)

★ The emoticon ":–)" <u>is used to express</u> a smile. (表示被用來做…)

To V₁ / V₁-ing... (+ Aux) + be / V₂

說明 :

　　由於動詞不可以直接當作主詞，須將動詞改為不定詞或是動名詞之後才能視為名詞使用。當動名詞或不定詞作為主詞時，視為單數，後面要接單數動詞。例如文中：<u>raising insects for food has</u> little negative impact... ，動詞用 has。

★ <u>Exercising regularly helps</u> you keep fit and healthy.

★ <u>To know</u> is one thing while to do is another.

✚ 字彙補給站

1. **expert** (*n.*) 專家，行家

   With his professional skills, David is recognized as an expert in the mechanics.

2. **suggest** (*v.*) 建議

   Experts suggest that we should exercise at least 30 minutes every day to maintain our health.

3. **especially** (*adv.*) 尤其

   Mandy likes fruits, especially mangos, and bananas.

4. **convenience** (*n.*) 方便

   Some people pay with credit cards due to its convenience.

5. **demand** (*n.*) 要求；需求

   The demand for electricity tends to increase in the summertime.

6. **estimate** (*v.*) 估計；評估

   It was estimated that over fifty thousand people were involved in the countdown party this year.

7. **consumer** (*n.*) 消費者

   This survey indicates the consumers' attitude toward the use of credit cards.

8. **thirsty** (*adj.*) 口渴的

   After two-hour working on the farm, Kevin felt so thirsty that he wanted nothing but a bottle of iced water.

9. **negative** (*adj.*) 消極的

   The politician has a negative attitude toward the election result.

10. **environment** (*n.*) 環境

    The air pollution will damage not only our health but (also) the environment.

➕ 文法加油站

1

Because of + N, ...

Because + S + V, ...

說明：

此句型表示「由於…；因為」，because of 後要接名詞或名詞片語，而 because 後則接完整子句，例如文中：Because of the convenience, there is a huge demand...。

★ The supermarket is crowded with people because of a big sale.

= The supermarket is crowded with people because there is a big sale.

★ Because of the heavy rain, the baseball game was canceled.

= Because it rained heavily, the baseball game was canceled.

2

祈使句

說明：

此句型表示「請求、命令、勸告或禁止」的句子。使用祈使句時，是向「對方」下達命令，或要求「對方」做事，所以主詞是 you (你或你們)。只不過在使用祈使句時，主詞通常都會省略，因此祈使句開頭才以「原型動詞」的形式出現。例如文中：So the next time you buy a bottle of water, think about the negative effect it has on our planet. Try to bring your own bottle and be friendly to our environment!

★ Work out with me at the gym.

★ Look at the blackboard and turn to page 30.

▶ **Part 1**

The Impossible Burger

Do you know that meat-free burgers have been making a comeback lately owing to the rise in popularity of vegetarian and vegan diets? Veggie burgers have always been considered a bit boring and lacking in flavor __1__ the real thing. However, innovative vegetarian chefs are starting to __2__ that concept of burgers that is winning over meat lovers and food critics alike. Now there's even a new kind of burger that looks, tastes and smells exactly the same __3__ a beef burger. The Impossible Burger __4__ was developed by Impossible Foods Inc., even "bleeds" like a regular cow-based burger. The exact recipe is, of course, a closely guarded secret, but the company does reveal on its website that the Impossible Burger contains "simple __5__ found in nature," including wheat, coconut oil and potatoes. Maybe next time you can try to make your own veggie burgers at home.

_____ 1.(A) combined with   (B) compared with

      (C) contributed to   (D) communicated to

_____ 2.(A) deny   (B) afford   (C) remove   (D) change

_____ 3.(A) as   (B) of   (C) with   (D) about

_____ 4.(A) that   (B) whom   (C) , which   (D) , who

_____ 5.(A) ingredients   (B) vitamins   (C) mysteries   (D) insects

▶ **Part 2**

Photobomb: Making Boring Photos Better

Have you ever taken a picture and later noticed someone funny or strange who was not supposed to be in the photo? If so, you've been photobombed! It is neither about ghost stories nor about unknown mysteries. Photobombing can be done __1__, such as pulling a funny face behind someone taking a selfie. However, there are many instances when someone is photobombed by accident. Photobombers don't have to be people. __2__, some of the funniest examples of photobombing involve animals. One famous photobomb is of a couple __3__ by a lake. They __4__ their camera to take a photo of themselves using a timer. Just __5__ the camera took the shot, a chipmunk, a cute animal like a squirrel, popped up right in front of the camera. What a classic photobomb!

_____ 1. (A) on purpose   (B) with caution   (C) in use   (D) in return

_____ 2. (A) As a result   (B) In fact   (C) In addition   (D) Briefly speaking

_____ 3. (A) sat   (B) to sit   (C) sitting   (D) from sitting

_____ 4. (A) are setting up   (B) are set up   (C) had set up   (D) had been set up

_____ 5. (A) because   (B) although   (C) after   (D) when

➕ 字彙補給站

1. **owing to** 由於；因為

   The baseball game was forced to stop owing to the heavy rain.

2. **vegetarian** (*n.*) 素食者

   Mandy has been a vegetarian for five years due to some health reasons.

3. **consider** (*v.*) 認為

   People with obesity (肥胖症) are considered to be a high-risk group of cardiovascular disease (心血管疾病).

4. **flavor** (*n.*) (食物或飲料的)味道

   Which flavor of ice cream would you like?

5. **innovative** (*adj.*) 創意的；創新的

   With his innovative design, Frank came in first place in the hairdo contest.

6. **concept** (*n.*) 概念

   The original concept of the scientist was proven correct.

7. **win over** 說服

   Alice will do her best at the audition (試鏡) to win over the film director.

8. **critic** (*n.*) 批評家；評論家

   David suggested me not to read the critic's article about the film before watching it.

9. **recipe** (*n.*) 食譜

   Linda has a special recipe for apple pie, which is popular among the neighbors.

10. **reveal** (*v.*) 透漏；洩漏

    The manager refused to reveal any details about the meeting.

➕ 文法加油站

---

1 **S + V + O + OC**

說明：

此句型為不完全及物動詞，包括 consider、believe、find、think 等思考型動詞，其受詞補語大多為形容詞或名詞(片語)，意思為「認為…是…」。而文中：Veggie burgers have always been <u>considered</u> a bit boring and lacking...，因 veggie burgers 被認為無趣、滋味不夠，故用 be considered + Adj.。

★ The woman <u>believes</u> herself a genius.

★ Hank <u>considered</u> himself very lucky.

---

2 **N, who / whom / which...,**

說明：

此句型為非限定用法的關係子句，主要用在<u>補充說明</u>先行詞，也稱為<u>補述</u>用法的關係子句。當先行詞已明確不需要界定或指認 (也就是<u>唯一情況</u>)，或是為<u>專有名詞</u> (人名、地名) 時，便會使用非限定用法的關係子句。例如文中：The Impossible Burger, <u>which</u> was developed by Impossible Foods Inc., even "bleeds" like...，非限定的關係子句有四個重點：① 關係代名詞之前必須有逗號。② 關係代名詞不可以用 that。③ 關係代名詞不可以省略。④ 在非限定用法的關係子句上，非限定關係代名詞 which 還可指稱前述的一整件事，而不是單指子句前面的那個字。

★ David lied to his girlfriend again, <u>which drove her crazy</u>.

   (這邊的先行詞指的是前面 David 欺騙女友這整件事情。)

★ Taipei 101, <u>which is the tallest building in Taiwan</u>, attracts a lot of tourists every year.

   (先行詞 Taipei 101 相當明確而且也只有一個，這裡的關係子句只是補充說明 Taipei 101 的訊息，所以用補述用法。)

➕ 字彙補給站

1. **notice** (*v.*) 注意；察覺

   William focused on his work and did not notice the lunch time.

2. **be supposed to** 應該；應當

   Lily was supposed to arrive home at 6:00 p.m.

3. **photobomb** (*v.*) (拍照時)亂入，搶鏡

   The naughty boy liked to photobomb when his sister took a selfie.

4. **mystery** (*n.*) 神祕的事物

   The private <u>detective</u> (偵探) solved the mystery of the murder at the end of this novel.

5. **selfie** (*n.*) 自拍

   A series of selfies were posted by Kevin on his Facebook yesterday.

6. **instance** (*n.*) 例子；情況

   Can you give me some more instances of <u>discrimination</u> (歧視) in the workplace?

7. **by accident** 偶然；意外地

   Emily broke the dish by accident. She didn't mean to do it.

8. **involve** (*v.*) 包含；包括；牽涉其中

   This job involves a lot of interviews with the consumers, so we need people with good communicative skills.

9. **pop up** 突然出現

   Anna's boyfriend popped up and gave her a bunch of flowers.

10. **in front of** 在…前

    I couldn't get out of the room because the man stood in front of the door.

➕ 文法加油站

N + who / which / that + V... → N + V-ing

說明：

　　此句型為限定用法的關係子句簡化為分詞片語的用法。當關係代名詞 (who、which、that) 是主格時，可以將關係子句簡化為分詞片語，來修飾先行詞。例如文中：One famous photobomb is of a couple sitting by a lake... (= One famous photobomb is of a couple who sat by a lake...)，依據動詞的主動或被動，關係子句可簡化為現在分詞片語 (V-ing) 或是過去分詞片語 (Vpp)。

★ The girl who is talking to Peter is my young sister.

　= The girl talking to Peter is my young sister. (女孩交談是主動的)

★ The students who were chosen to join the basketball team were over 175 cm tall.

　= The students chosen to join to the basketball team were over 175 cm tall. (學生是被選出來的)

從屬連接詞 after, before, when, while, because, although

說明：

　　從屬連接詞所在的子句稱為從屬子句，其不能獨立存在，它是用來說明主要子句，需與主要子句連用。根據語意可分為表示「時間」、「原因」、「讓步」的從屬子句，例如文中：Just when the camera took the shot, a chipmunk, a cute animal like a squirrel, popped up right in front of the camera 的 when 表示「當…時候」。當從屬子句放於主要子句之前，中間會有逗點隔開。

★ Although he was poor, he was happy.

★ Because there is no space on the desk, I put the cake on the chair.

▶ Part 1

Selfies with New Technology

These days people are taking selfies as never before, but the way that people are taking selfies is changing. Instead of simply holding the cell phone with their hands and ___1___ "cheese," people take a photo of themselves with selfie sticks. Over the past few years, selfie sticks have grown in popularity ___2___ they offer a greater variety in terms of shot angle, number of people in the shot, and so on. But what is the next stage in the evolution of selfies? It's the selfie drone! Drones are small devices that fly around like mini helicopters. ___3___ the user carries a simple tracking device with themselves, a selfie drone can follow it and serve as a "personal photographer." You could, for example, ski down a hill while ___4___ selfie drone automatically follows along taking photos or videos of you. While selfie drones certainly don't come cheap, the cost ___5___ come down as the market grows. If you're interested in this new technology, you may wait for a perfect price!

_____ 1.(A) say   (B) says   (C) said   (D) saying

_____ 2.(A) as   (B) before   (C) though   (D) if

_____ 3.(A) Even if   (B) As long as   (C) Even as   (D) Although

_____ 4.(A) you   (B) your   (C) yours   (D) yourself

_____ 5.(A) is sure to   (B) is uncertain to   (C) is unable to   (D) be used to

▶ *Part 2*

The Food with Strong Smell

There are many dishes around the world which have a reputation for having a strong smell or taste that many people find it a little disgusting. Take stinky tofu __1__ . Its powerful smell often proves too much for many foreigners. Even some of the more __2__ foreign visitors in Taiwan are not even willing to try a bite of stinky tofu due to its odd smell. __3__ challenging dish is from Norway—Lutefisk. It is a dish __4__ white fish that is dried in the air. It smells really __5__ and has a unique jelly-like texture that is difficult to describe and even harder to swallow! Not only do foreign visitors find lutefisk a rather unpleasant dish but many locals also admit they don't like it. Next time you visit there, would you dare to try it?

_____ 1.(A) for instance   (B) for granted

     (C) as reference   (D) into consideration

_____ 2.(A) innocent   (B) adventurous   (C) diligent   (D) significant

_____ 3.(A) One   (B) Other   (C) Another   (D) The other

_____ 4.(A) which made from   (B) made from

     (C) that is making from   (D) which is to make

_____ 5.(A) badly   (B) ugly   (C) awful   (D) terrific

➕ 字彙補給站

1. **technology** (*n.*) 科技

   With technology, people live a more convenient life than before.

2. **popularity** (*n.*) 流行；受歡迎

   The LOHAS goods gain much popularity as more and more people are willing to be friendly to our environment.

3. **offer** (*v.*) 提供

   Because the breakfast is not offered in the hotel tomorrow, we need to buy some bread in advance.

4. **variety** (*n.*) 變化；多樣性

   The teacher advised that there should be more variety in my composition.

5. **in terms of** 在…方面

   In terms of effectiveness, the new version of iRobot still doesn't meet my needs.

6. **evolution** (*n.*) 進化；演化

   The book mainly talks about the evolution of aboriginal languages in Taiwan.

7. **helicopter** (*n.*) 直升機

   The visitors have a sightseeing tour of the city by helicopter.

8. **photographer** (*n.*) 攝影師

   Ann is a talented musician as well as a professional fashion photographer.

9. **automatically** (*adv.*) 自動地

   When you press the button, the washing machine will work automatically and all the laundry will be done in one hour.

10. **come down** (價格或水準)下降

    The price of vegetables has come down because the supply is greater than demand.

➕ 文法加油站

1   Instead of + N / V₁-ing, S + V₂...

說明：

　　此句型表示「不是⋯，而是⋯」，instead of 為介系詞片語，其後需接名詞或動名詞。例如文中：Instead of simply holding the cell phone with their hands and saying "cheese," people take a photo of themselves with selfie sticks.

★ Albert will go to the library instead of the museum.

★ Instead of staying at home, Lisa went out shopping with her friends last night.

2   If + S + V..., S + Aux + V...

說明：

　　此句型表示「假如⋯」，為 if 直說法條件句，表示對未來的預測，其結果有可能發生。其中含有 if 的子句稱為「條件子句」，不含 if 的稱為「主要子句」，用以表示結果。If 引導的條件子句中的動詞時態為現在簡單式，主要子句則根據語意使用 can, may, shall, should, will 等助動詞 (Aux)。需注意的是即使 if 引導的條件子句表示未來的情況，該子句的時態仍用現在簡單式。例如文中：If you're interested in this new technology, you may wait for a perfect price!。

★ Brian should have a balanced diet and take exercise if he wants to lose weight.

★ If it rains tomorrow, we won't go on a picnic in the park.

➕ 字彙補給站

1. **reputation** (*n.*) 名聲，名氣

   This hotel has a good reputation for its excellent service and beef noodles.

2. **disgusting** (*adj.*) 噁心的

   It was too disgusting for me to try "Balut (鴨仔蛋)," a dish from Southeast Asia.

3. **powerful** (*adj.*) 強烈的

   Some people don't like durian because of its powerful smell.

4. **foreigner** (*n.*) 外國人

   Talking with foreigners is one of the ways that you can practice foreign languages.

5. **willing** (*adj.*) 樂意(做某事)

   Ruby is an enthusiastic person, and I think she will be willing to help.

6. **odd** (*adj.*) 奇怪的

   It's odd that Jane behaved rudely today. She used to be a polite person.

7. **texture** (*n.*) 口感

   We can't resist the handmade cookies because of its crispy texture.

8. **describe** (*v.*) 描述

   The police asked the witness to describe what he had seen at the scene.

9. **admit** (*v.*) 承認

   No officials are willing to admit their mistakes in the policy.

10. **Not only... but (also)** 不僅⋯而且

    The director not only writes his own plays, but acts in them.

➕ 文法加油站

1

S have a reputation for + 特色 / V-ing
S have a reputation as + 身分 / 地位

說明：

　　此句型表示「以…聞名；以…著稱」，注意 for 之後接的是使其有名的特色，as 之後接的是使其有名的身分、地位…等等。例如文中：There are many dishes around the world which have a reputation for having a strong smell or taste... (特色是有強烈的味道)。

★Sun Moon Lake has a reputation for its beautiful scenery. (特色是其美麗的景色)

★Taipei 101 has a reputation as the tallest building in Taiwan. (以台灣最高樓聞名)

2

S + leave / keep / find + O + OC (Adj / V-ing / Vpp)

說明：

　　此句型中 keep 及 leave 表示「使某人 / 某物保持…狀態」，而 find 為「覺得某人 / 某物…或是發現某人 / 某物處於…狀態」，其皆為不完全及物動詞，因加上受詞 (O) 後句意仍不完整，故其後須再接受詞補語 (OC)，來補充說明受詞的狀態。一般常見的受詞補語有形容詞 (Adj)、現在分詞 (V-ing；表主動) 或過去分詞 (Vpp；表被動)。例如文中：...taste that many people find it a little disgusting.。

★Grace did not find her purse stolen until she got home. (被動)

★Please keep the window open.(open *adj.* 打開的；開著的)

The Fog Catcher

In many parts of the world, the annual rainfall is very low. The Atacama Desert in Chile, South America, is particularly dry, so the people living there are having trouble __1__ enough water. __2__ the lack of rain, there is water contained in clouds that blow in from the coast. This often creates a thick fog over the mountains. Unfortunately, the drops of water in the fog are __3__ tiny __3__ they don't fall out of the air. In order to solve the problem, scientists have developed special nets __4__ fog catchers which trap these drops of water. The holes in the nets are tiny, __5__ just 1 mm across. The fog catching system is cheap, easy to maintain, and provides plenty of water for local residents.

_____1.(A) to get   (B) getting   (C) being got   (D) getting with

_____2.(A) Beside   (B) Due to   (C) Despite   (D) As a result of

_____3.(A) too...to...   (B) such...that...   (C) so...that   (D) very...that

_____4.(A) called   (B) calling   (C) that called   (D) which call

_____5.(A) measuring   (B) producing   (C) connecting   (D) importing

The Effect of Climate Change on the Earth

The impact of climate change has been found around the world. One obvious ___1___ is the rising sea level, caused by the increasing temperature and melting glaciers. This phenomenon actually makes many tourist attractions ___2___ with people. For example, the number of tourists visiting Glacier National Park in the USA has hit a record high recently. It is predicted that by 2030 all of the glaciers in the park ___3___ completely melted. This has led many tourists to come to see the remaining glaciers before they disappear ___4___. A similar situation also occurs in Venice, one of the famous cities in Italy. In spite of having taken some measures, the Italian government still can't help Venice remove the ___5___ from rising sea levels. As a result, Venice has been crowded with tourists all over the world. But in addition to visiting these endangered tourist attractions as soon as possible, what else can people do when facing the impact of climate change?

_____ 1.(A) effect   (B) presence   (C) reaction   (D) input

_____ 2.(A) flood   (B) flooded   (C) flooding   (D) to be flooding

_____ 3.(A) are   (B) have   (C) had   (D) will have

_____ 4.(A) as well   (B) for good   (C) in season   (D) at times

_____ 5.(A) security   (B) expectation   (C) religion   (D) threat

➕ 字彙補給站

1. **annual** (*adj.*) 每年的；一年一次的

   Our annual school carnival (園遊會) takes place in June for school anniversary celebration.

2. **rainfall** (*n.*) 下雨；降雨量

   If we don't receive a good rainfall this month, we will face a water crisis.

3. **desert** (*n.*) 沙漠

   Because of the lack of rain, it is difficult to grow crops in the desert.

4. **particularly** (*adv.*) 特別；尤其是

   Rita is interested in the challenging games, particularly the jigsaw puzzles (拼圖).

5. **contain** (*v.*) 包含

   A healthy diet usually contains lots of fruits and vegetables.

6. **thick** (*adj.*) 厚的

   It's weird that the man wears a thick jacket in this hot weather.

7. **trap** (*v.*) 收集；保存

   The scientists use solar panels (太陽能電板) to trap energy from the sun.

8. **maintain** (*v.*) 維持；保養

   It was dangerous for children to play in the playground because it was poorly maintained.

9. **plenty** (*pron.*) 大量

   Plenty of friends will go to Dan's birthday party.

10. **resident** (*n.*) 居民；住戶

    This gym is only for the residents of the building to work out. It is not open to the public.

➕ 文法加油站

> ### 1　S + have + difficulty / trouble / a hard time (in) + V-ing

說明：

此句型表示「在…方面有困難；難以…」，其中介係詞 in 常被省略，後面加動名詞 (V-ing)。例如文中：the people living there are having trouble (in) getting enough water.。

★ Peter had difficulty (in) getting along with others because of his bad temper.

★ Wendy had a hard time (in) adapting herself to the foreign culture when she studied abroad.

> ### 2　S + V... + in order to / so as to + V...

說明：

此句型表示「為了…」，其後接原形動詞表示「結果」或「目的」。用法如下：

⑴ in order to 可以放在句中或句首，so as to 只能放在句中。

⑵ in order to + V 可省略為 to + V。

例如文中：In order to solve the problem, scientists have developed special nets...。

★ Oliver got up early this morning so as to catch the first train to Taipei.

★ In order to win the contest, Tim practices singing two hours a day.

➕ 字彙補給站

1. **climate** (*n.*) 氣候

   Taiwan is an island country whose climate is mild but humid.

2. **obvious** (*adj.*) 顯然的；明顯的

   Peter looked very sleepy this morning and it was obvious that he didn't sleep well last night.

3. **temperature** (*n.*) 溫度

   Don't wash your sweater at a high temperature or it will shrink.

4. **melt** (*v.*) 融化

   The ice cream melted quickly in the hot weather, and made my hands dirty.

5. **phenomenon** (*n.*) 現象

   Rainbows are a natural phenomenon.

6. **attraction** (*n.*) 嚮往的地方；觀光景點

   Ben will go to Paris to visit all the famous tourist attractions such as the Eiffel Tower and the Louvre Museum.

7. **remaining** (*adj.*) 剩餘的；其餘的

   Daisy decided to donate her remaining income to the charity groups.

8. **disappear** (*v.*) 消失

   A figure flashed by the window and disappeared in the dark.

9. **measure** (*n.*) 措施；方法

   The measure is designed to solve the traffic jam and will be tried next month.

10. **endanger** (*v.*) 危及；使…處於危險之中

    Not following the traffic rules endangers your own safety as well as others'.

➕ 文法加油站

1

make + O + OC (Adj / N)

說明：

此句型表示「使…變得…」、「使…覺得…」以及「使…成為…」，其中的 make 為不完全及物動詞，後接受詞 (O) 時，須有受詞補語 (OC) 對受詞作補充說明，而受詞補語多為形容詞或名詞。 例如文中： This phenomenon actually makes many tourist attractions flooded with people.，句中 flooded 是形容詞，表示「充斥…的」，本句語意為「這個現象事實上使得很多觀光景點充斥著人群」。

★ Singing always makes me happy.

★ The movie made the actress a superstar.

2

in spite of + V-ing, S + V...

說明：

此句型表示「儘管…」之意，由於 in spite of 為介係詞，故後面應接名詞或動名詞，不可直接加上句子，相同意思及用法還有 despite。 例如文中： In spite of having taken some measures, the Italian government still...。若要接子句，其後必須先接名詞 the fact，再用 that 引導該子句。

★ In spite of her young age, the girl has won the women's golf championship.

★ In spite of the fact that John and his sister work for the same company, they don't see each other very often.

▶ **Part 1**

A Rare Moment of Peace—the Christmas Truce

On Christmas Day, 1914, something unusual happened. Germany __1__ at war with Britain for nearly five months. Thousands of soldiers on both sides were being killed and __2__ every day. The soldiers were tired and missed their loved ones back in their home countries. Although they couldn't help but do their duty to help win the war, they would have much preferred to stop __3__. And that's just what happened on Christmas Day, at least for a short time. Some soldiers took a break from the daily task of shooting __4__ the enemy to have a soccer match right there on the battlefield. Today, friendly soccer matches __5__ around the world at Christmas to remember this special moment of peace during World War I. People can also visit the Christmas truce statue at St. Luke's Church in Liverpool, which shows a German soldier and a British soldier shaking hands over a football.

_____ 1.(A) is   (B) was   (C) has been   (D) had been

_____ 2.(A) excited   (B) satisfied   (C) injured   (D) adopted

_____ 3.(A) fighting   (B) by fighting   (C) to fight   (D) for fighting

_____ 4.(A) in   (B) at   (C) with   (D) by

_____ 5.(A) stay up   (B) back up   (C) take effect   (D) take place

Internship Makes You Stronger

Many students go traveling in their summer vacation. But, some apply for a student internship to gain valuable work experience __1__ some funds. In fact, many businesses also actively seek summer interns through the Internet or the schools. __2__ those who used to be student interns, there are three major advantages for your future career. One advantage is learning about an industry. Being an intern, you can have more chance to know __3__ . Another good point as an intern is increasing your strengths. As a professional intern with a good interpersonal relationship, you will be more __4__ to be hired while seeking employment later. __5__ advantage of being an intern is getting you more qualified at school. Many schools recognize the value of internships and give course credits. So, if you don't have plans for the approaching summer vacation, why not give it a try?

_____ 1.(A) as long as   (B) as well as   (C) as soon as   (D) as far as

_____ 2.(A) Speaking of   (B) Regardless of   (C) According to   (D) Except for

_____ 3.(A) what an organization is like   (B) what is like an organization

     (C) how an organization is like   (D) how like is an organization

_____ 4.(A) costly   (B) likely   (C) friendly   (D) lovely

_____ 5.(A) Other   (B) Another   (C) The other   (D) The others

字彙補給站

1. **duty** (*n.*) 責任，義務

   It was Alice's duty to take good care of her children.

2. **prefer** (*v.*) 偏好

   The man prefers drinking black coffee in the morning.

3. **daily** (*adj.*) 日常的

   By making exercise a part of your daily routine, you will have a healthier life.

4. **task** (*n.*) 任務

   David was given a task of helping the refugees rebuild their houses.

5. **the enemy** (*n.*) 敵軍

   Our troops have broken through the lines of the enemy, and won the victory over.

6. **match** (*n.*) 比賽

   Eventually, Rita won the tennis match.

7. **battlefield** (*n.*) 戰場，戰地

   As a war correspondent (戰地記者), Frank reported the latest news from the battlefield.

8. **friendly** (*adj.*) 友好的

   Amada has a lot of friends because she is friendly to others.

9. **statue** (*n.*) 雕像

   The Statue of Liberty is a landmark of New York City.

10. **injured** (*adj.*) 受傷的

    The man couldn't walk by himself because his knee was badly injured.

✚ 文法加油站

S + can't help but + V / can' help + V-ing

說明 :

　　此句型表示「忍不住…；不得不…；不由得…」，can't help but 後加原形動詞，
例如文中 ： Although they <u>couldn't help but do</u> their duty to help win the war, ... ，而
can't help 後加動名詞。

★ I <u>couldn't help but wonder</u> Judy's words because she looked uneasy.

★ The woman <u>couldn't help crying</u> when she knew her son was dying.

something / anything / nothing / everything + Adj

說明 :

　　此為後位修飾。一般來說，形容詞會放在要修飾的名詞之前，但複合代名詞如
something / anything / nothing / everything 或 somebody / anybody / nobody /
everybody 或 someone / anyone / no one / everyone 等代名詞的前面已經含有一個限
定詞 some, any 等 ， 所以修飾它的形容詞要<u>放在後面</u> 。 例如文中 ： ...<u>something
unusual</u> happened. 。

★ Did you notice <u>anything special</u> in the morning?

★ The police asked the old woman if there had been <u>someone strange</u> coming here.

➕ 字彙補給站

1. **internship** (*n.*) 實習期

   More and more students have a summer internship in big companies, putting their knowledge into practice.

2. **apply** (*v.*) 申請

   If you want to use the study room in the library, you need to apply for permission.

3. **gain** (*v.*) 取得

   The woman gained rapid promotion by working hard.

4. **valuable** (*adj.*) 珍貴的

   It was a valuable experience for Jenny to study overseas.

5. **fund** (*n.*) 資金

   The charity has set up a fund to help the victims of the earthquake.

6. **advantage** (*n.*) 優勢；優點

   The advantage of booking tickets in advance is that you'll have a seat in your trip.

7. **strength** (*n.*) 優點；優勢

   One of Susan's strengths is her determination. Once she makes a decision, she will achieve her goal no matter how difficult it is.

8. **professional** (*adj.*) 專業的

   They are not professional singers but their voice was clear and strong.

9. **seek** (*v.*) 尋找

   Hundreds of students are seeking for a job after graduation.

10. **qualified** (*adj.*) 有資格的

    Sally was quite qualified for this job and got an offer immediately.

文法加油站

1

through + N, ...

說明 ：

此句型表示「透過…；藉由…的方式」，through 為介係詞，其後要接名詞或 V-ing 。 例如文中 ：...many businesses appreciate and actively seek summer interns through the Internet or the schools. 。

★ Amanda finally achieved success through her hard work.

★ The fire fighter rescued the children from the blaze through a ladder.

2

One, another, the other...

說明 ：

此句表示有三個對象時「一…，另一…，還有一…」，One, another 和 the other 都是不定代名詞，用來代替前面已經提過的名詞。它們也可以當不定形容詞，其中 one (一個) 跟 another (另一) 後面必定接單數名詞跟單數動詞 。 例如文中 ：...there are three major advantages for your future career. One advantage is learning about an industry. Another good point as an intern is increasing your strengths...The other advantage of being an intern is getting you more qualified at school. 。

★ The student drew the picture with three colors. One is red, another is blue and the other is yellow.

★ Josh ate three pies. One was apple, another was banana and the other was mango.

▶ **Part 1**

A Clearing in the Rainforest

Rainforest plays an important role in maintaining global climate. Unfortunately, people __1__ 200,000 square kilometers of rainforest around the world every year. That's an area about five and a half times the size of Taiwan. The problem is even worse in Brazil and Indonesia. __2__, it seems that the two nations are in competition with each other to see which country can cut down its rainforests faster. In the past, Brazil was the clear winner, __3__ down huge areas of rainforest at a quicker rate than Indonesia. However, Indonesia has increased its forest-clearing __4__ and has now overtaken Brazil. The winner of this contest is the owners of the companies who make big __5__ from the wood they sell. Who are the losers? Every plant, animal, and human being living on this planet.

_____ 1.(A) criticize   (B) ignore   (C) destroy   (D) signal

_____ 2.(A) In fact   (B) However   (C) Therefore   (D) Thus

_____ 3.(A) cut   (B) cuts   (C) to cut   (D) cutting

_____ 4.(A) efforts   (B) calendars   (C) careers   (D) glances

_____ 5.(A) threats   (B) profits   (C) resources   (D) habitats

The "Talkies"

Do you love movies? A lot of people do. Then, some facts about movies must arouse your interest. First __1__ , movies were in black and white and soundless. In many of these silent movies, words appear on the screen to provide the audience __2__ information about the story. Moreover, movie theaters hired musicians to perform during the film. The type of music played __3__ the scene on the screen. Slower music was used for the sad or romantic scenes, and quicker, lively music for comedy and action scenes. As __4__ improved, movies with sound came out. The audience could hear not only sounds but the actors talking. These new movies were thus called "talkies." People were too surprised to believe it was true. Some people even considered talkies a stupid idea. __5__ , time has proven them wrong. This fantastic change has made movies more popular.

_____ 1.(A) invent   (B) invented   (C) inventing   (D) to invent

_____ 2.(A) in   (B) at   (C) for   (D) with

_____ 3.(A) resulted in   (B) looked into   (C) depended on   (D) searched for

_____ 4.(A) recovery   (B) technology   (C) target   (D) recipe

_____ 5.(A) Particularly   (B) Globally   (C) Obviously   (D) Hardly

字彙補給站

1. **rainforest** (*n.*) (熱帶) 雨林

   The rainforests cover only 6% of the Earth's surface, but many plant and animal species are still found there.

2. **play an important role in...** 在某事上扮演重要角色

   Parental love plays an important role in helping children grow happily.

3. **maintain** (*v.*) 維持，保持

   In order to maintain the oil prices, the OPEC made a decision to reduce the amount of oil.

4. **kilometer** (*n.*) 公尺

   The total area of the Yellowstone National Park is about 8,991 square kilometers.

5. **in competition with** 與…競爭，角逐

   The restaurant is in competition with not only other local restaurants but also overseas ones.

6. **rate** (*n.*) 速率；速度

   Seeing Greg's rapid rate of progress after the surgery, his parents sighed with relief.

7. **increase** (*v.*) 增加

   As we know, staying up late constantly increases the risk of illness.

8. **overtake** (*v.*) 超越

   It is very dangerous to overtake other vehicles at will.

9. **contest** (*n.*) 比賽

   Kate made up her mind to take part in the speech contest.

10. **loser** (*n.*) 失敗者

    Being a good loser is the hardest thing to learn.

➕ 文法加油站

1   **It seems that S + V**

說明：

　　此句型當中的 seem 為連綴動詞，常用來表示「看起來、似乎、好像」之意。

★ It seems that Larry doesn't pay much attention to his schoolwork.

★ It seems that Kate has nothing to do with this case.

2   **S + have / has + Vpp**

說明：

　　此句型為現在完成式可表示 ① 從以前持續到現在的動作。 ②曾經有過的經驗。③ 動作的完成。例如文中：However, Indonesia has increased its forest-clearing...，即為從以前持續到現在的動作。

★ Daisy has been to Japan for three times. (曾有過的經驗)

★ Lucy has handed in the report. (動作的完成)

✚ 字彙補給站

1. **arouse** (*v.*) 引起，激起

   Mr. Lin usually designs activities to arouse students' interest.

2. **silent** (*adj.*) 沉默的

   The naughty boys became silent when their teacher appeared.

3. **provide** (*v.*) 提供

   The charity is here to provide the homeless with food and drink.

4. **audience** (*n.*) 觀眾，聽眾

   The performance was so terrific that the audience clapped loudly.

5. **moreover** (*adv.*) 此外 (= besides; in addition)

   Peggy enjoys the cooking class, and moreover, she likes the friends there.

6. **romantic** (*adj.*) 浪漫的

   With soft music and candlelight, the couple is enjoying a romantic dinner.

7. **comedy** (*n.*) 喜劇

   A Midsummer Night's Dream, written in earlier years, is one of Shakespeare's most famous comedies.

8. **scene** (*n.*) 場景

   The touching scene in the movie moved me to tears.

9. **obviously** (*adv.*) 明顯地，顯然

   Vincent has a crush on Betty, but obviously he won't admit.

10. **fantastic** (*adj.*) 極好的

    It's a fantastic achievement for David to reach the final of the national singing contest.

➕ 文法加油站

Vpp..., S + V...

說明：

此句型為被動的分詞構句。將副詞子句改成被動的分詞構句有以下三步驟：

(1) 省略連接詞 (when, while, before, after 亦可留著)。

(2) 前後子句的主詞一樣，則省略主詞。

(3) 將動詞改成過去分詞 Vpp (此為被動)。

★ When Jimmy was asked why he was late again, he said nothing.

　→ (When) Asked why he was late again, Jimmy said nothing.

★ When Helen was called by the teacher, she was laughing.

　→ (When) Called by the teacher, Helen was laughing.

too + Adj / Adv (+ for sb.) + to V

說明：

此句型表示「太⋯以致於不能⋯」，too 後面可以接形容詞或副詞，而 to 後則須接原型動詞，例如文中：People were <u>too surprised to believe</u> it was true.。

★ Daisy is <u>too shy to speak</u> in front of the whole class.

★ Kelly ran <u>too slowly to catch</u> the bus.

> ▶ **Part 1**

Getting Married in a Unique Way

Getting married is one of the most important events in a person's life. Most couples want to have a religious wedding __1__ and wear traditional wedding clothes. However, more and more couples these days are choosing to have a non-traditional wedding. Some ideas are __2__ crazy that they may make your jaw drop. For example, there are couples __3__ the knot while jumping out of planes, standing at the bottom of the ocean, wearing Halloween costumes, flying in a hot air balloon, you name it. In fact, people have got married in almost every way you can think of. One wedding was reported to __4__ at a Starbucks. What's more surprising, another was held at a beach __5__ everyone, including the wedding guests, was completely naked. Who knows? Perhaps this passage will inspire you to get married in a unique way one day!

_____ 1.(A) identity   (B) background   (C) ceremony   (D) captain

_____ 2.(A) very   (B) so   (C) too   (D) such

_____ 3.(A) tying   (B) tie   (C) to tie   (D) to be tied

_____ 4.(A) take place   (B) take off   (C) take effect   (D) take cover

_____ 5.(A) how   (B) that   (C) where   (D) which

Special Christmas Events

December 25th is a day of celebration in many countries around the world. However, Christmas traditions are not certainly limited to December 25th. Many activities __1__ Christmas occur on January 5th, which is the twelfth and final day of the Christmas period. __2__ decorating Christmas trees and giving presents, what else do Westerners do? In Germany, __3__, it is the custom for children to leave a shoe outside their bedroom door before going to bed at night. In the morning, they will find their shoe __4__ of candy. In France, people share a traditional kind of cake called a king cake. Inside a king cake, there is a small figure. Whoever gets a piece of cake containing the figure will become "king" or "queen" and have the __5__ of wearing a fancy paper crown. It goes without saying that each child hopes he or she will be the lucky one.

_____ 1.(A) popular with   (B) ashamed of   (C) associated with   (D) capable of

_____ 2.(A) Because of   (B) Out of   (C) In spite of   (D) In addition to

_____ 3.(A) for example   (B) such as   (C) as a result   (D) above all

_____ 4.(A) filled   (B) full   (C) to fill   (D) be full

_____ 5.(A) vacancy   (B) honor   (C) appearance   (D) weight

字彙補給站

1. **couple** (*n.*) 夫妻；情侶

   The couple were falling in love with each other at first sight, and they quickly decided to get married.

2. **religious** (*adj.*) 宗教的

   Larry is very interested in some religious services in Taiwan.

3. **traditional** (*adj.*) 傳統的

   It is traditional for Taiwanese to give children red envelopes on Lunar New Year's Eve.

4. **jaw** (*n.*) 下巴

   The police arrested the drunk for punching others on the jaw.

5. **knot** (*n.*) 結

   Gary is trying to teach his little brother how to tie a ribbon in a knot.

6. **completely** (*adv.*) 完全地

   Mark has completely changed his attitude after he learned his lesson.

7. **naked** (*adj.*) 赤裸的

   Some people like to sleep naked because they think it can make them feel freer and happier.

8. **passage** (*n.*) 章節；段落

   Some of the lines from this movie are a short passage from the Bible.

9. **inspire** (*v.*) 給予靈感；激發

   This fantastic scenery inspired Susan to create such beautiful music.

10. **unique** (*adj.*) 獨特的

    It is David's belief that each of his students is unique.

🟦 文法加油站

1　one of the Adj-est + N

說明：

此句型表示「最⋯其中之一」，為形容詞最高級的用法。最高級形容詞前加上定冠詞 the，且後方的名詞須為複數名詞。形容詞若為單音節，則在字尾加 -est；若為多音節，則保留原形，並在前面加上 the most，例如文中：Getting married is one of the most important events in a person's life.。

★ Angelina Jolie is one of the prettiest actresses in the world.

★ Maldives is one of the most popular attractions for honeymoon trips.

2　make / let / have + O + V (主動的動作)

說明：

此句型表示「使、讓 (強迫)」，make、let、have 為使役動詞。若使役動詞後面的受詞是主動的用法，則後面可省略 to，直接用原型動詞。例如文中：Some ideas are so crazy that they may make your jaw drop.，此句的 drop 為主動。

★ Jeff's mom made him clean up his room.

★ Tim's boss made him do a marketing project.

字彙補給站

1. **celebration** (*n.*) 慶祝；慶祝活動

   The celebrations for the Lantern Festival at the town always attract tens of thousands of visitors every year.

2. **tradition** (*n.*) 傳統

   Wearing new clothes and setting firecrackers are the traditions of Chinese New Year.

3. **limit** (*v.*) 侷限，限制

   The doctor suggested that Victor limit himself to one cup of coffee a day.

4. **activity** (*n.*) 活動

   Our teacher designed many interactive classroom activities for us to do in class, such as role play or Think-Pair-Share.

5. **occur** (*v.*) 發生

   Since a terrible murder occurred in the house, it has become deserted.

6. **final** (*adj.*) 最終的

   Dr. Lee gave his patient a final warning of smoking.

7. **custom** (*n.*) 習俗

   It's better to know the local culture and customs when we travel abroad.

8. **figure** (*n.*) 人偶；身影

   The figure of lion was a gift from my father.

9. **crown** (*n.*) 王冠

   In ancient Greece, people wove the laurel leaves into a crown as a symbol of victory and honor.

10. **fancy** (*adj.*) 昂貴的；奢華的

    We don't have enough money to stay in the fancy hotel even for one night.

文法加油站

in addition to + V-ing / N

說明 :

　　此句型表示「除…外還有…」，將後面的人 / 事 / 物包含在內，用於附加說明，例如文中： In addition to decorating Christmas trees and giving presents...，此片語也可用 besides 來代換。

★ In addition to (= Besides) pizza, Gary had a hamburger and pasta for dinner.

★ In addition to (= Besides) giving me some advice, Jerry also gave me some money.

whoever　 = anyone who

whatever　 = anything that

whichever = any / either of them that

說明 :

　　此為複合關係代名詞，是由關係代名詞加上字尾 -ever。相當於先行詞 + 關係代名詞 (如上述 whoever = anyone who) ，所以前面不需要先行詞 ，例如文中： Whoever (= Anyone who) gets a piece of cake containing the figure will become...。

★ The teacher asked his students to choose whichever topic (= any of the topics that) they like to do their reports.

★ Since Gary has lied to Jane many times, she won't believe whatever (= anything that) he says.

▶ **Part 1**

A Fun Way to Test Your Knowledge of Physics

It's time to test your knowledge of physics! When it comes to building bridges, what materials do you think would make a strong __1__? Stone? Good answer. Metal? Even better. How about uncooked spaghetti? Wonderful! Although it may sound strange, many university engineering departments hold contests __2__ students must design and build a "spaghetti bridge." It is a little bridge __3__ entirely of uncooked spaghetti and glue. There are many rules, but at one university, the bridge must be built across a gap measuring 40 centimeters. The bridge __4__ can support the heaviest weight in the middle for five seconds is the winner. The contest is a __5__ and fun way to test many aspects of students' engineering knowledge, such as pressure, angles, forces, and so on. Does it make you interested in trying to build one yourself?

_____ 1.(A) structure   (B) planet   (C) ambition   (D) impression

_____ 2.(A) that   (B) which   (C) how   (D) in which

_____ 3.(A) made   (B) making   (C) which made   (D) which making

_____ 4.(A) where   (B) that   (C) who   (D) whose

_____ 5.(A) chemical   (B) following   (C) unique   (D) royal

Get Enough Sleep

What is the modern lifestyle like? Working or studying long hours is now a normal part of life in modern society. As a result, it is common that people are too busy to get enough sleep. However, long-term lack of sleep is now being recognized __1__ a serious health risk factor. Fifty years ago, doctors realized the harmful effect that smoking can have on one's health and started recommending that people __2__ smoking. __3__ believe that we are now in a similar position when it comes to sleep. Studies show that even short-term lack of sleep __4__ blood pressure and influences blood sugar. Obesity and mood problems have also been linked to too little sleep. Of course, the amount of sleep we need varies from person to person, but __5__, less than six hours' sleep per night is considered very unhealthy. So, for the sake of health, we had better get sufficient sleep even if we are terribly busy.

_____ 1.(A) in   (B) as   (C) at   (D) with

_____ 2.(A) quit   (B) quits   (C) quitted   (D) quitting

_____ 3.(A) Politicians   (B) Customers   (C) Applicants   (D) Researchers

_____ 4.(A) raises   (B) appeals   (C) debates   (D) permits

_____ 5.(A) no longer   (B) on the contrary

     (C) at once   (D) generally speaking

➕ 字彙補給站

1. **knowledge** (*n.*) 知識

   Without professional knowledge, you cannot perfectly fit yourself for the job.

2. **physics** (*n.*) 物理

   According to the laws of physics, nothing can travel faster than light.

3. **material** (*n.*) 材料

   Wood is the only material for the great building.

4. **university** (*n.*) 大學

   It was hard for women to study at university over one hundred years ago.

5. **engineering** (*n.*) 工程 (學)

   Harry decided to major in engineering in college.

6. **design** (*v.*) 設計

   The picture books are designed for kindergarten children.

7. **entirely** (*adv.*) 完全地

   Mark devotes himself entirely to social work after retiring.

8. **gap** (*n.*) 開口，裂口

   Judy cares a lot about the gap between her front teeth.

9. **pressure** (*n.*) 壓力

   Kate has trouble sleeping due to great work pressure.

10. **and so on** 等等

    The shop at the corner sells a wide variety of things, such as clothes, shoes, hats, and so on.

➕ 文法加油站

It is time to + V

說明：

此句型表示「現在是時候做某事了」，若後面加 to，則須接原形動詞，例如文中：It is time to test your knowledge of physics! 另外，It is time 後面若接名詞，則需用 for 作介係詞，如 It is time for + N。

★ It is time to take a break.

★ It is time for lunch.

When it comes to + 人 / 事物 / V-ing, S + V

說明：

此句型表示「每當提到」，指在談話或撰寫時，談論到某主題，並藉此表達對此主題的態度及看法。When 所帶出的句子可放在句首或句尾。例如文中：When it comes to building bridges, what materials do you think would make a strong structure?。

★ When it comes to playing basketball, Leon is all thumbs.

★ Tim is an absolute genius when it comes to architecture.

✚ 字彙補給站

1. **modern** (*adj.*) 現代的

   With the advance of modern technology, we can now live a more convenient life.

2. **normal** (*adj.*) 正常的，典型的

   The woman's blood pressure was higher than normal after she worked out for 30 minutes.

3. **long-term** (*adj.*) 長期的

   Long-term illness has made the man depressed and bad-tempered.

4. **lack** (*n.*) 缺乏

   The woman failed to get the job for lack of working experience.

5. **recognize** (*v.*) 認定

   The bakery is recognized as the best in the town.

6. **factor** (*n.*) 因素

   There are two important factors of Jason's success. One is hard work, and the other is good luck.

7. **realize** (*v.*) 意識到

   Dan didn't realize that he had broken Nancy's heart with some offensive remarks.

8. **harmful** (*adj.*) 害人的

   Smoking is harmful to your health, so you must quit it.

9. **obesity** (*n.*) 肥胖

   The boy has to eat a healthier diet and exercise more to fight obesity.

10. **sufficient** (*adj.*) 充足的

    Daisy is not sure if she has sufficient time to prepare for the party.

➕ 文法加油站

1 recommend / suggest / advise / propose... + that S + (should) + V

說明：

此句型表示「建議」，為意志動詞的用法，其後的 that 子句，常省略助動詞 should，因此子句會用原形動詞。例如文中：...and started recommending that people quit smoking.

★ The doctor advised that Oscar (should) cut down on meat and exercise more.

★ The teacher suggested that the students (should) study hard.

2 had better + V

說明：

此片語表示「最好…」，可將其視為助動詞，故其後接原形動詞。例如文中：...we had better get sufficient sleep...。若是否定，則為 had better not。

★ Andrew had better hand in his report on time, or he might be flunked.

★ Bill had better not cheat on the test. It does no good to him at all.

▶ **Part 1**

Internet Security

In the Information Age, we are increasingly dependent on the Internet both for work and for our personal lives. In this way, information __1__ is a big concern. There are numerous horror stories of people __2__ identities have been stolen by hackers. Needless to say, __3__ is necessary to have a very strong password. Unfortunately, all your passwords can be easily stolen by special computer viruses. That is __4__ some web services like Google and Facebook recommend using a two-step password. Step 1 __5__ entering your password in the normal way. For step 2, you need to enter a number sent by text message to your cell phone. This makes it much harder for hackers to get into your online accounts. After all, you can't be too careful.

_____ 1.(A) device   (B) security   (C) tendency   (D) faith

_____ 2.(A) who   (B) when   (C) which   (D) whose

_____ 3.(A) it   (B) that   (C) what   (D) which

_____ 4.(A) what   (B) where   (C) why   (D) how

_____ 5.(A) involves   (B) absorbs   (C) appreciates   (D) constructs

The Reading Barber

As we know, reading plays an essential role in our life. It can make our life much richer. It goes without saying that this good habit should be __1__ in childhood, for the ability to read is one of the key parts of a child's education. Some kids take to reading naturally like ducks to water. A barber in the U.S. state of Michigan has __2__ a novel idea to encourage local elementary school children to read more. Kids who read out loud __3__ having their hair cut can get a $2 discount. It's a win-win-win for the barber, the parents, and the children. __4__ word about the project spreads, people in the neighborhood were inspired to donate books. Since the awesome plan was started, there __5__ countless kids joining in. Those lucky children not only have a less expensive haircut but also get a most valuable treasure of life—reading.

_____ 1.(A) developed   (B) debated   (C) declined   (D) declared

_____ 2.(A) got rid of   (B) cut down on   (C) run out of   (D) come up with

_____ 3.(A) and   (B) because   (C) while   (D) though

_____ 4.(A) As   (B) Though   (C) Even if   (D) Because of

_____ 5.(A) had been   (B) have been   (C) has been   (D) was been

字彙補給站

1. **Internet** (*n.*) 網路

   Nowadays, it's convenient for people to buy daily commodities on the Internet.

2. **dependent** (*adj.*) 依靠的，依賴的

   The student is dependent on the scholarship.

3. **personal** (*adj.*) 私人的

   It's rude to ask personal questions such as one's age.

4. **concern** (*n.*) 擔心或關心的事

   Food safety is one of the major concerns in Taiwan.

5. **numerous** (*adj.*) 許多的

   After numerous attempts, Ben finally has the chance to fulfill his dream.

6. **horror** (*n.*) 恐怖；驚恐

   Kate cried out in horror when seeing a cockroach in the kitchen.

7. **recommend** (*v.*) 建議

   The doctor recommended that Steve should quit smoking and exercise more.

8. **normal** (*adj.*) 正常的；普通的

   Although Emily gets the flu, her temperature is still normal.

9. **account** (*n.*) 帳號，帳戶

   Josh couldn't believe his email account had been hacked twice.

10. **after all** 畢竟

    We have to study hard; after all, we're still students now.

➕ 文法加油站

have / has been + Vpp

說明：

此句型為現在完成被動式，如同現在完成式可表示 ① 從以前持續到現在的動作。② 曾有過的經驗。③ 動作的完成，只是動作為被動。例如文中：...identities have been stolen by hackers.。

★ Peter has been punished several times for being late for school. (曾有過的經驗)

★ Thanks to Molly's help, my application has been accepted. (動作的完成)

It + be + Adj + to V

說明：

此句型的使用時機一般是句中主詞過長時，為避免句子頭重腳輕，會將過長的主詞移至句子後半部，並用虛主詞 it 來引導整個句子，例如文中：It is necessary to have a very strong password.。

★ It is illegal to drive a car without a license.

★ It is good for health to have a balanced diet and enough sleep.

字彙補給站

1. **essential** (*adj.*) 必要的，重要的

   Having good English speaking ability is essential for the job.

2. **habit** (*n.*) 習慣

   With a good eating habit, you will have a healthier life.

3. **childhood** (*n.*) 童年

   Gary spent his childhood in this small town with his grandparents.

4. **take to** 開始從事；形成…的習慣

   Just like her father, Anna took to drawing at an early age.

5. **novel** (*adj.*) 新奇的

   Scott is an interesting person with novel ideas.

6. **encourage** (*v.*) 鼓勵

   Vivian treats her students patiently and always encourages them.

7. **discount** (*n.*) 折扣

   You will get a special discount by clicking the like button on our Facebook.

8. **spread** (*v.*) 傳播

   The disease spread so fast that the government had to take immediate measures.

9. **neighborhood** (*n.*) 街坊

   The man used to live in a poor neighborhood but now he is a successful businessman.

10. **valuable** (*adj.*) 寶貴的

    Every moment I spent with my family is valuable for me.

文法加油站

It goes without saying that S + V

說明 ：

此句型表示「不用說 (大家都知道)」，例如文中：It goes without saying that this good habit should be developed in childhood... ，亦可寫成 It is needless to say that S + V，更可以再簡化成 Needless to say, S + V。

★ It goes without saying that health is much more important than wealth.

★ It is needless to say that Wesley will try his best to achieve his goal.

★ Needless to say, exercising regularly is the best way to lose weight.

not only + A + but (also) + B

說明 ：

此句型表示「不但 A 而且 B」，為對等連接詞，所以 A 和 B 必須詞類相同，且 also 可省略。例如文中： Those lucky children not only have a less expensive haircut but (also) get a most valuable treasure of life... (連接兩個動詞)；另外若連接兩個名詞作主詞時，則其後所接的動詞須配合 B。

★ Jonathan is not only smart but (also) diligent. (連接兩個形容詞)

★ Not only the students but (also) the teacher likes the activity. (動詞 like 須配合 the teacher，故用第三人稱單數)

▶ **Part 1**

The Midas Touch

In English, the phrase "the Midas touch" means that someone has a talent for making money. The expression comes from a Greek myth about a king __1__ Midas who was given a special power by a god. __2__ this gift he was able to turn anything he wanted into gold just by touching it. At first, the king was __3__ with his new-found ability and greedily turned many objects into gold. He was so overjoyed that he ran to his daughter to hug her. However, __4__ he touched her, she was transformed into solid gold, too. He was frightened and tried every possible way to turn his daughter back. __5__ hard he tried, he couldn't change her back. He didn't realize that his gift was in fact a curse until then. Although he had become the richest, yet he was the unhappiest man in the world.

_____ 1.(A) named   (B) naming   (C) who named   (D) who naming

_____ 2.(A) In   (B) At   (C) About   (D) With

_____ 3.(A) confused   (B) delighted   (C) annoyed   (D) frustrated

_____ 4.(A) even though   (B) as if   (C) in spite of   (D) as soon as

_____ 5.(A) No matter what   (B) No matter when

       (C) No matter how   (D) No matter who

The Urban Legend

Have you ever heard of "urban legends?" Urban legends are stories on the Internet about something very unusual, surprising or amazing. They are called legends because they are well-known stories usually __1__, or they may just be partly true. Here is a good example of urban legends. __2__ is said that Walt Disney, the founder of the Walt Disney Company, planned to have his head frozen after death. He hoped that scientists would one day be able to bring him back to life. It's a classic urban legend still believed to be true despite all the __3__ showing it is nonsense. Stories like these are fun to read, but before sharing them with your friends online, you had better __4__ they are not urban legends. That is, avoid __5__ yourself. Otherwise, you may become a laughing stock among your friends.

_____ 1.(A) burst out   (B) made up   (C) set out   (D) used up

_____ 2.(A) It   (B) That   (C) What   (D) Which

_____ 3.(A) peace   (B) harvest   (C) evidence   (D) challenge

_____ 4.(A) lead to   (B) make sure   (C) major in   (D) dress up

_____ 5.(A) embarrass   (B) embarrassed   (C) to embarrass   (D) embarrassing

✚ 字彙補給站

1. **talent** (*n.*) 天賦

   Mozart had a talent for music.

2. **expression** (*n.*) 說法

   "Overweight" is a more polite expression than "fat."

3. **myth** (*n.*) 神話

   According to Greek myth, Athena represents wisdom, craft and war.

4. **object** (*n.*) 物體

   Students are asked to be very careful with every object in the laboratory.

5. **overjoyed** (*adj.*) 欣喜若狂的

   All the people of the country were overjoyed to hear the prince's wedding announcement.

6. **transform** (*v.*) 使改變

   The sudden change in the family transformed Adam into a totally different person.

7. **solid** (*adj.*) 固體的

   When water freezes, it becomes solid.

8. **frightened** (*adj.*) 受驚嚇的

   The little kid got frightened and cried when the room turned dark suddenly.

9. **in fact** 事實上

   The little boy told his mother he would go to the library, but in fact, he went to play with his friends.

10. **curse** (*n.*) 詛咒

    A prince broke the curse by giving the princess a kiss at the end of the story.

✚ 文法加油站

as soon as + S + V, S + V

說明：

此句型表示「一…就…」，連接幾乎同時發生的兩個動作，as soon as 為從屬連接詞，引導副詞子句。例如文中：However, as soon as he touched her, ...。

★ The phone rang as soon as I got home.

★ As soon as Larry saw the teacher, he stopped talking.

S + V + so + Adj / Adv + that + S + V

說明：

此句型表示「如此…以致於…」，因此可知前後文具有因果關係。so 是副詞，後面可接形容詞或副詞，而 that 則為連接詞，引導子句。例如文中：He was so overjoyed that he ran to his daughter to hug her.。

★ The student was so tired that he fell asleep on the bus and missed his stop.

★ The skirt is so small that the girl can't wear it.

字彙補給站

1. **urban** (*adj.*) 都市的

   Urban life is so busy that Julie feels like getting away from it.

2. **legend** (*n.*) 傳說

   Legend has it that if you make a wish upon a shooting star, the wish will come true.

3. **well-known** (*adj.*) 眾所皆知的

   As a well-known saying goes, "Honesty is the best policy."

4. **founder** (*n.*) 創辦人

   The founder of this technology company retired at the age of 90.

5. **freeze** (*v.*) (使) 凍結

   The lake is completely frozen due to the extreme climate.

6. **despite** (*prep.*) 儘管 (= in spite of)

   Jessie quit her job despite her parents' disagreement.

7. **nonsense** (*n.*) 謬論；愚蠢的想法

   Whenever Matt starts to talk nonsense, Dana just goes away.

8. **avoid** (*v.*) 避免

   Ken usually avoids going shopping at Costco on weekends because it's so crowded.

9. **otherwise** (*adv.*) 否則

   You must do your best. Otherwise, you have no chance of winning.

10. **laughing stock** 笑柄

    If you do that, you will make yourself a laughing stock.

➕ 文法加油站

1

It is said that + S + V

說明：

此句型表示「據說」，還可以寫成：S + be + said + to V，另外句型中的 said 可以因文意需求而變為 believed, reported, thought, considered, estimated。例如文中：It is said that Walt Disney, ...。

★ It is said that Anna is good at gardening. (據說)

　→ Anna is said to be good at gardening.

★ It is reported that a typhoon is coming next week. (據報導)

　→ A typhoon is reported to come next week.

2

when / while / before / after 引導的副詞子句改為分詞構句

說明：

副詞子句改為分詞構句，其步驟為 ① 這四個連接詞可省略，亦可保留。② 前後主詞一樣，須省略主詞。③ 將動詞改成現在分詞 (主動)。例如文中：..., but before sharing them with your friends online, you had better... (原句為：..., but before you share them with your friends online, you had better...)

★ After Iris studied for two hours, she took a break.

　→(After) Studying for two hours, Iris took a break.

★ When I shopped at the supermarket, I met my teacher.

　→ (When) Shopping at the supermarket, I met my teacher.

▶ **Part 1**

It's Not All About Making Money

Sometimes, I like to take a trip to the City Zoo. We have an amazing zoo full of __1__ from around the world and the staff do fantastic jobs making efforts to take care of them. __2__ at these animals makes me reflect on why we have zoos. One of the main reasons is to entertain people for profit. Visitors come to watch the animals eating, playing and getting around. And going to the zoo may be the only chance to see a real lion or a giraffe __3__ you travel to Africa. But actually it's not all about making money. Zoos do help __4__ endangered species. They also educate and inspire people to care more about and look after our planet for the future __5__. So next time when you go to a zoo, give more thought about what you can do for animals.

_____ 1.(A) creatures   (B) careers   (C) decorations   (D) degrees

_____ 2.(A) Look   (B) Looks   (C) Looked   (D) Looking

_____ 3.(A) because   (B) unless   (C) though   (D) meanwhile

_____ 4.(A) protect   (B) protects   (C) protected   (D) protecting

_____ 5.(A) symbols   (B) descriptions   (C) journeys   (D) generations

Laughing Makes You Better

Studies have shown that laughing every day helps the body stay fit and healthy. It also helps patients get better much more quickly. Here at the London Laughter Club, we certainly believe that to be true. Laughing is also a kind of ___1___ exercise, helping you to keep a joyful, stress-free and positive attitude toward life. The most ___2___ comes from laughing long and hard but that's not easy to achieve by yourself. That's why we gather in large groups on a daily basis to laugh with our experienced "Laugh Leaders" ___3___ aside. Come and join us! The first time is completely free. If you feel shy, ___4___ with a friend! Check us out on the web at *londonlaughterclub.net*. We are ___5___ your coming. Do grab this good chance to become healthier and happier. Not until you really join us will you know what will happen to you.

_____ 1.(A) mental   (B) upset   (C) digital   (D) curious

_____ 2.(A) opportunity   (B) leisure   (C) flood   (D) advantage

_____ 3.(A) to guide   (B) guiding   (C) guide   (D) guided

_____ 4.(A) came   (B) coming   (C) come   (D) to come

_____ 5.(A) relying on   (B) carrying out

      (C) putting up with   (D) looking forward to

字彙補給站

1. **staff** (*n.*) 員工

   The whole staff in the company are asked not to work overtime.

2. **effort** (*n.*) 試圖

   The man made an effort to stop smoking and started exercising for his health.

3. **reflect** (*v.*) 認真思考，沉思

   The man paused for a moment, and said he needed time to reflect.

4. **entertain** (*v.*) 娛樂

   Frank often entertains his parents with jokes.

5. **profit** (*n.*) 利潤

   After years of low profits, the convenience store couldn't help but close down.

6. **visitor** (*n.*) 遊客，訪客

   Jack went to the door to receive his visitors from New York.

7. **endangered** (*adj.*) 瀕臨絕種的

   It is reported that polar bears have become endangered.

8. **species** (*n.*) 物種

   How many species of trees are there in the forest?

9. **inspire** (*v.*) 激勵；鼓舞

   Martin Luther King's speech inspired people to strive for the rights of equality.

10. **look after** 照顧 (= take care of)

    Ruth decided to drop out of school to look after her sick mother.

➕ 文法加油站

1   S + V + 疑問詞 (why / what / how / when / where / who / whom) + S (+ Aux) + V

說明：

　　此句型為以疑問詞為首所引導的名詞子句，又稱為「間接問句」，即在一個主要子句中包含疑問子句作名詞使用。若要將直接問句改間接問句須注意以下四點：

⑴ 助動詞 do / does / did 須省略，但若是否定句，則保留。另須注意，省略此助動詞後，普通動詞改回該有的時態。

⑵ 除了 do / does / did 之外的助動詞 will, should, can, may, ... 等則不省略。

⑶ 恢復 S + V (主詞在前，動詞在後) 的順序。

⑷ 句尾的標點符號，視主要子句做改變。

例如文中：...on why we have zoos. (直接問句：Why do we have zoos?)；...thought about what you can do for animals. (直接問句：What can you do for animals?)。

★ Can you tell me how Tom finished the job? (直接問句：How did Tom finish the job?)

★ I have no idea when Jane will go to Taipei. (直接問句：When will Jane go to Taipei?)

2   S + see / watch / hear /listen to + O + V / V-ing

說明：

　　此句型為感官動詞的用法，若感官動詞之後的動作為主動發出動作者，受詞後可接原形動詞或現在分詞。用現在分詞強調該動作正在進行；若接原形動詞，則著重於陳述事實。例如文中：Visitors come to watch the animals eating, playing and getting around. (主動的動作)。

★ The boy saw a bird fly / flying in the sky.

★ Brenda hears her daughter practice / practicing the piano every day.

✚ 字彙補給站

1. **healthy** (*adj.*) 健康的

   Eating more fruits and vegetables is one of the tips for staying fit and healthy.

2. **patient** (*n.*) 病人

   The patient is still recovering from the heart surgery.

3. **joyful** (*adj.*) 高興的

   I'm glad to hear this joyful news that Mark got a job as an editor in a publishing company.

4. **stress-free** (*adj.*) 無壓力的

   The teacher designed a stress-free activity in which each student could talk about whatever they want.

5. **positive** (*adj.*) 積極的；正面的

   We should always be positive and look on the bright side.

6. **attitude** (*n.*) 態度，看法

   Gordon's bad attitude made his boss very upset.

7. **achieve** (*v.*) 達到

   Only by working hard may we achieve success.

8. **gather** (*v.*) 聚集

   Children were gathering around the ice cream stall, waiting to buy ice cream.

9. **on a daily basis** (*adv.*) 每日地 (= every day)

   Although Robert is terribly busy, he works out in the gym on a daily basis.

10. **grab** (*v.*) 抓取

    The man tried to grab the woman's handbag from her but he failed.

✚ 文法加油站

1

$$S + V_1, \text{ and (S)} + V_2 \rightarrow S + V_1, V_2\text{-ing}$$

說明：

　　將對等子句改成主動的分詞構句，有以下兩個步驟 ① 去連接詞 and。② 將 V_2 改成現在分詞。例如文中：...laughing is also a kind of mental exercise, <u>helping</u> you to keep a joyful... (此句原為：...laughing is also a kind of mental exercise, and (it) helps you to keep a joyful...)。

★ Phoebe waved at me and said goodbye. → Phoebe waved at me, <u>saying</u> goodbye.

★ Richard rode his bike and sang happily. → Richard rode his bike, <u>singing</u> happily.

2

Not until + S + V + Aux + S + V

說明：

　　此句型為 not...until... 的進階寫法，"not...until" 表示「直到…才…」，其連接的兩個子句時態須一致。另外，until 之後也可接一個時間點。若要將 not until + S + V 放句首，後面 (主要子句) 的主詞和動詞要倒裝。例如文中：Not until you really join us <u>will you</u> know what will happen to you. (此句原為：You will not know what will happen to you until you really join us.)。

★ Not until midnight <u>did Martin</u> get home.

　　→ Martin didn't get home until midnight.

★ Not until the teacher explained again <u>did Harry</u> understand the key point.

　　→ Harry didn't understand the key point until the teacher explained again.

20分鐘稱霸統測
英文對話

劉妃欽、莊靜軒／編著

- 十五回單元設計，完整收錄近年共 60 個統測對話必考情境。
- 獨家主題式情境對話編寫並搭配跨頁圖解實用句，使讀者身歷其境，學習效果加倍。
- 版面編排活潑配合中文翻譯，方便讀者完整對照。
- 豐富的小知識補充及英語加油站，增進知識提升英語能力，完整瞄準統測對話延伸學習。
- 全新撰寫的單元試題測驗對話熟悉度，並附歷屆試題掌握統測出題脈絡。
- 獨家附贈對話手冊，完整蒐集日常生活及統測實用問答句，重點迅速複習。

108課綱
贏戰統測

20分鐘
稱霸統測
英文
綜合測驗

解析本

莊靜軒、蕭美玲　編著

- 面對分秒必爭的考生生活，你該如何分配時間？
- 面對各式各樣的考試內容，你該如何抓住重點？

每天 20 分鐘，快速練習統測英文綜合測驗

東大圖書公司

Contents

中譯：

　　電梯的由來可以一直回溯至羅馬時代，奴隸拉繩讓平台在樓層間升高或降低。直到 1823 年第一座蒸氣驅動的電梯才問世。兩位英國建築師發明蒸氣驅動的「升降室」，帶觀光客到能俯瞰倫敦美景的高台。稍晚的設計讓大樓電梯變得更大更好。然而，卻有一個主要的缺點：非常不安全。所幸，1852 年時，伊萊莎·奧的斯發明一種新型電梯來解決安全問題。奧的斯電梯的關鍵特色是防電梯摔落的安全裝置。時至今日，奧的斯電梯公司仍舊是全球最大電梯製造商之一，連艾菲爾鐵塔和日本首座摩天樓等知名建築，都裝有奧的斯電梯。

解析：

B 1.此句型為 It be 被強調的部分 that...，目的是強調句中的某部分，強調的部分不可為動詞，此句強調時間「not until 1823」。⇨ ✚ **文法加油站 1**

A 2.此題先行詞為 platform，在形容詞子句 (關係子句) 中是一地點，故答案選 (A) 關係副詞 where。若要用關係副詞 which 的話，須將介係詞 on 保留。例如文中：a high platform <u>where</u> they could enjoy a view of London = a high platform <u>on</u> <u>which</u> they could enjoy a view of London.

C 3.前述在說明電梯越改越好的情況，而後述點出缺點，所以此用轉折語氣，故答案選 (C) However 然而，(A) Therefore 因此 (B) Surprisingly 意外地 (D) Furthermore 此外，皆不符語意。

B 4.(A) hide (*v.*) 隱藏 (B) solve (*v.*) 解決 (C) support (*v.*) 支持 (D) interrupt (*v.*) 中斷

D 5.此語意為「防電梯摔落…」，而 prevent / keep / stop...from + N / V-ing 表示預防 / 避免 / 阻止…做…，所以選 (D) from。

中譯：

　　玩具一直是人類文化的一部分。雖然許多現代玩具已經很難讓過去的孩子認出來，但也有一些玩具，幾世紀以來人氣不減。玩具名人堂座落於紐約。那是個搜集古往今來經典玩具的博物館。其中包括大家熟悉的玩具，例如泡泡、風箏、球和紙牌。此外，也有一般不會被視為玩具的日常物品，像是厚紙箱、毯子和木棍。小孩子在這似乎不管拿到任何東西，都能變做玩具或發明玩法。只要一點想像力，身邊的任何東西都能帶來數小時的樂趣。這座博物館確實值得造訪，所以如果你到紐約玩，別錯過了。

解析：

B 1.此題語意為「雖然許多現代玩具已經很難讓過去的孩子認出來…」所以根據語意，本題選 (B) While 雖然，儘管。

D 2.此題考關係子句的概念，先行詞為 museum，關係代名詞是主格，故選 (D) which。

A 3.從 bubbles, kites, balls and playing cards 可知這些是常見的玩具，故根據語意選 (A) familiar (*adj.*) 熟悉的，其餘選項均不符合語意。(B) domestic (*adj.*) 國內的，本國的 (C) temporary (*adj.*) 暫時的 (D) commercial (*adj.*) 商業的。

C 4.從 cardboard boxes, blankets and sticks 可知這些東西是常見的物品，故本題選 (C) objects 物品。

D 5.此題語意為「只要一點想像力，身邊的任何東西都能帶來數小時的樂趣。」，故答案選 (D) with 有…的情況下。with + N 的句型，是用來引導一種情境或是表示一種原因，附帶說明主要句子的語意。⇨ ➕ **文法加油站 1**

Part 1 *It's Time to Start Eating Bugs Again*

中譯 :

　　據說現代人類約 12 萬 5 千年前離開非洲，進而逐漸分布全球。人類居住的地方，從熱帶雨林到繁華城市。於是，人類賴以存活的食物多樣化，並不令人意外。如今，現代飲食侷限於幾種穀物，例如小麥、玉米、稻米，以及幾種農場動物，像是牛、豬、雞。然而，人類以前幾乎無所不吃，包括蟲子在內。蟲子是優秀的蛋白質來源。此外，培育蟲子當食物，對環境幾無負面影響。許多人相信，為了健康和地球著想，我們應該再度開始吃蟲子。

解析 :

B 1. 此題是指人們居住範圍「從…到…」(from...to)，所以選 (B) to。

A 2. 此題空格 it 為虛主詞，表示 that 子句的這件事情，意思是「人類賴以存活的食物多樣化，並不令人意外。」

B 3. (A) positive (*adj.*) 正面的 (B) modern (*adj.*) 現代的 (C) complete (*adj.*) 完整的 (D) meaningful (*adj.*) 有意義的，此題從前面的 nowadays 來判斷，選 (B) 最適合。

A 4. 從本句的 that included insects 可知在描述過去人們食用的情形，所以選 (A) used to。

D 5. 此題為 S + have a(n)...impact on + N (對…有影響) 的句型，所以選 (D)。

Part 2 *Say "No" to Bottled Water*

中譯：

　　保健專家經常建議大家白天要喝足水，特別是天氣很熱的時候。由於便利，瓶裝水的需求很大。全球消費者估計每年花超過 1000 億美元買瓶裝水。雖然喝瓶裝水便宜又方便，但環境成本很高，因為塑膠瓶是石油化學產品。此外，將瓶裝水運給全球各地口渴的消費者，必須燒掉大量燃料。所以，下次你買瓶裝水，考慮這對我們的地球會有什麼樣負面影響。嘗試自備水瓶，友善對待我們的環境！

解析：

D 1. 此題語意為「⋯的需求」(...demand for + N)，故本題選 (D) for。

C 2. 此題 (A)～(C) 均為「花費」之意，英文裡根據主詞及花費的東西來決定動詞。

　　(1) 人　　　　　　spend 金錢 / 時間 ... (in) + V-ing / spend 金錢 / 時間 on sth.

　　(2) 事 (物)　　　　cost + (人) + 金錢

　　(3) 事 (物)　　　　take + (人) + 時間 / 精神 / 精力⋯

　　　　人　　　　　take 時間 to V...

　本題主詞為 consumers (人)，花費金錢，故選 (C) spend，(D) pay (*v.*) 付款則不合語意。

B 3. 此題前一句解釋瓶裝水方便又便宜,後一句點出其缺點耗費大量的環境成本,故根據語意選 (B) Though 雖然。

C 4. 此題前述瓶裝水造成環境損失，後又敘述運送瓶裝水耗費燃料，都是在說明瓶裝水的缺點，故本題選 (C) In addition 此外。

A 5. 此題最後為呼籲讀者思考瓶裝水對環境的影響，為祈使句。此句型為表示「請求、命令、勸告或禁止」的句子，主詞是第二人稱 You (你；你們)，但通常被省略，使用原形動詞，故答案選 (A) think about。⇨ ➕ **文法加油站 2**

Unit 3

Part 1 *The Impossible Burger*

中譯：

　　你知道由於素食和全素餐的盛行，無肉漢堡最近又捲土重來了嗎？和真的漢堡相比，大家一直認為素漢堡無趣、味道又差。然而愛創新的蔬食主廚轉換了漢堡的概念，同時贏得肉食愛好者和美食評鑑家的讚揚。現在甚至有種新漢堡，看起來、嚐起來、聞起來，都和牛肉漢堡沒兩樣。由不可能食品公司開發出來的「不可能的漢堡」甚至像一般牛肉漢堡一樣「流汁」。配方當然嚴密保管，但該公司在官網上透露，不可能漢堡內含「自然界的簡單食材」，包括小麥、椰子油和馬鈴薯。也許，下次你可以試試在家自製素漢堡。

解析：

B 1. 本句為分詞構句的用法，主詞 Veggie buggers 被拿來與 the real thing 做比較，兩者被拿來做比較時，可用 A be compared with / to B，故本題選 (B) compared with。

D 2. (A) deny (*v.*) 否認 (B) afford (*v.*) 買得起 (C) remove (*v.*) 移除 (D) change (*v.*) 改變

A 3. exactly the same as 表示「跟…一樣」。

C 4. 當先行詞已經相當明確不需要界定、指認或為<u>專有名詞</u> (人名地名) 時，便會使用非限定用法的關係子句，在關係代名詞前加逗號，而此處的先行詞 Impossible Burger 為專有名詞，已是特定的東西不須界定，故選 (C), which。

A 5. (A) ingredient (*n.*) 原料 (食材) (B) vitamin (*n.*) 維他命 (C) mystery (*n.*) 奧秘 (D) insect (*n.*) 昆蟲

中譯：

　　你曾經拍完照後，才發現不該出現在照片裡的搞笑怪咖嗎？如果有，那就是被搶鏡亂入了！這和鬼故事或神怪事件無關。亂入可以是故意為之，例如在自拍的人背後扮鬼臉。但也很多意外亂入的案例。亂入者不盡然侷限於人。事實上，部分最有趣的亂入和動物有關。有張知名亂入照是一對坐在湖畔的情侶拍的。他們架好相機，設用定時器自拍。相機按下快門時，一隻長相像松鼠的可愛花栗鼠剛巧在相機鏡頭前冒出頭。真是經典的亂入啊！

解析：

Ａ　1.(A) on purpose 故意地 (B) with caution 小心地 (C) in use 使用中 (D) in return 回報。根據文章語意，從下一句 However, ... by accident 這邊的 However 與 by accident 可知選擇 (A)。

Ｂ　2.(A) As a result 因此 (B) In fact 事實上 (C) In addition 此外還… (D) Briefly speaking 簡短來說。

Ｃ　3.此題的 ...a couple sitting by a lake.，此為 a couple who sat... 關係代名詞為主格時省略的分詞片語，對 couple 而言，sit 這個字是主動的，故使用 V-ing。
　　⇨ **✚ 文法加油站** 1

Ｃ　4.此題語意為「他們架好相機，設用定時器自拍。」，根據後面句子敘述，可知動詞時態用過去完成式，表示已經完成的動作，故本題選 (C) had set up。

Ｄ　5.(A) because 因為 (B) although 雖然 (C) after 在…之後 (D) when 當…時候，根據語意選 (D)。⇨ **✚ 文法加油站** 2

Unit 4

Part 1 *Selfies with New Technology*

中譯：

　　如今，大家愈來愈愛自拍，但人們自拍的方式正逐漸改變。他們不再徒手舉起手機，說「笑一個」，而是拿自拍棒拍照。過去幾年，自拍棒人氣愈來愈高，因為能有不同的拍照角度、入鏡人數更多等等。但下一階段的自拍會演變成什麼樣子呢？就是自拍用無人機！無人機是一種能像迷你直升機一樣四處飛的小型裝置。用戶只要隨身攜帶簡單的追蹤裝置，自拍無人機便可以擔任「個人攝影師」緊緊相隨。例如，你可以滑雪下坡，而你的自拍無人機將自動跟在身後，替你拍照或錄影。儘管自拍無人機不便宜，但市場成長後成本必然會下滑。如果你對這種新科技感興趣，可以等價錢合意時入手！

解析：

D 1.空格前的 and 為對等連接詞，對等連接詞是用來連接句子中的字、片語或子句，其兩端必須是對等的。而本題 and 前為動名詞 holding，因此可以得知空格須填和 holding 對等的動詞，故此題選 (D) saying。

A 2.(A) as 因為 (B) before 在…之前 (C) though 雖然 (D) if 假如，此題語意為「自拍棒人氣愈來愈高，因為能有不同的拍照角度…」，故本題選 (A)。

B 3.(A) Even if 即使 (B) As long as 只要 (C) Even as 正當 (D) Although 儘管。其語意為「只要隨身攜帶簡單的追蹤裝置，自拍無人機便…」，可知選 (B)。

B 4.空格後為名詞 selfie drone 可得知空格應填所有格 (B) 或 (C)，而選項 (C) 為所有格代名詞，故此題應選 (B) your。

A 5.此題語意為「儘管自拍無人機不便宜，但市場成長後成本必然會下滑。」，所以答案選 (A) is sure to 必定…。

中譯 :

　　全球各地有許多菜餚因為帶有讓人食不下嚥的濃烈味道出名。以臭豆腐為例。臭味薰天經常讓外國人招架不住。即使是在臺灣一些較具冒險犯難精神的外國人，也因為臭豆腐的怪味，不敢一試。另一道挑戰度高的菜餚是挪威菜鹹漬魚。這道菜用曬乾的鱈魚製成。味道很刺鼻，具有難形容、更難入口的獨特果凍口感！不僅外國訪客覺得鹹漬魚不討喜，連許多本地人也承認並不喜歡它。下次你造訪挪威，敢不敢放膽一試？

解析 :

A 1.(A) Take...for instance 舉⋯為例 (B) Take...for granted 視⋯為理所當然 (C) Take...as reference 將⋯做為參考 (D) Take...into consideration 考慮⋯ ，根據前述，這邊要舉臭豆腐為例子，故本題選 (A)。

B 2.根據此句中的 try (嘗試) 以及前後文意，可推知願意嘗試的通常是需有冒險精神的人所以選 (B) adventurous 有冒險精神的；大膽的。

C 3.此篇文章談論世界上特殊難以下嚥的食物，前面先舉臭豆腐為例，接著再另外舉例，並未有特別指定的對象，故根據語意選 (C) Another。

B 4.此句原為 It is a dish which is made from white fish...，關係代名詞為關係子句的主格時可省略，故本題選分詞片語 (B) made from 由⋯製成。

C 5.此題 smell 為連綴動詞，之後要接形容詞，根據其後的 difficult to describe and even harder to swallow，可知選 (C) awful。

Unit 5

中譯：

　　世上有許多地方，年降雨量稀少。南美智利的阿塔卡馬沙漠尤其乾燥，所以住在那裡的人難以取得足夠的用水。儘管欠缺降雨，但從海岸吹拂過來的雲朵含有水氣。這經常使山區籠罩濃霧。不幸的是，霧裡的水滴是如此細微以致於無法自空中飄雨而下。為了解決這個問題，科學家研發出能收集這些霧水的特殊捕霧網。網洞細微，僅 1 公釐。捕霧系統很便宜，易於維護，為當地居民提供了足量用水。

解析：

B 1. 此題為 S + have trouble (in) + V-ing，表示「難以…；做…有困難」，in 可省略，故選 (B)。⇨ **➕ 文法加油站 1**

C 2. (A) beside 在…旁邊 (B) due to 因為還… (C) despite 儘管 (D) as a result of 由於。此題意為儘管缺雨，但自海岸吹拂過來的雲朵含有水氣，所以根據語意選 (C)。

C 3. (A) too...to... 太…而不能…，to 之後會接動詞。(B) such... that 如此…以致於，such 之後除形容詞之外還接名詞。(D) very...that 無此用法，故選 (C) so...that，語意為「霧裡的水滴是如此細微以致於無法自空中飄雨而下。」

A 4. ...special nets called fog catchers，此為 which is called... 關係代名詞為主格時省略的分詞片語，nets 是被稱為 fog catchers (被動)，故使用 Vpp。

A 5. (A) measure (*v.*) 有… (長、寬、高) 的大小 (B) produce (*v.*) 製造 (C) connect (*v.*) 連接 (D) import (*v.*) 進口，輸入

中譯：

　　氣候變遷的影響在全球各地都看得到。由於氣溫升高、冰河融化，顯而易見的是海平面上升。這個現象其實使人潮湧入許多觀光景點。例如，造訪美國冰川國家公園的訪客人數最近創下空前紀錄。這個國家公園裡的所有冰河預估將在 2030 年前全部消融。這導致大批觀光客趕在冰川永遠消失之前，前來一睹殘存風貌。義大利的知名城市威尼斯也有類似情況。雖然採取了一些措施，但義大利政府仍無法幫助威尼斯躲過海平面上升的威脅。於是，來自全球各地的觀光客將威尼斯擠得水洩不通。但除了儘快造訪這些瀕危景點外，人們面臨氣候變遷的衝擊，還能有何作為？

解析：

A 1. 從第一句的 "impact" 可推知，延續前述氣候變遷的影響，故此題選 (A) effect (*n.*) 影響，(B) presence (*n.*) 存在 (C) reaction (*n.*) 反應 (D) input (*n.*) 輸入，均不合語意。

B 2. 此題為 make + O + OC，表示「使⋯變得⋯」，其受詞須有受詞補語作補充說明，而受詞補語多為形容詞或名詞，故選 (B) flooded (*adj.*) 大量⋯的；充斥⋯的。⇨ ➕ **文法加油站 1**

D 3. 此句語意為「⋯所有冰河預估將在 2030 年前全部消融。」，可得知其表示將持續到未來某一時間 (且可能會持續下去) 的動作，即為未來完成式。而未來完成式的句型為 shall / will + have + Vpp，故此題選 (D) will have。

B 4. 從前述 ...completely melted，故本題選 (B) for good 永遠地，(A) as well 也 (C) in season 當季 (D) at times 偶爾；有時候，均不合語意。

D 5. (A) security (*n.*) 安全 (B) expectation (*n.*) 期待 (C) religion (*n.*) 宗教 (D) threat (*n.*) 威脅

Unit 6

中譯 :

　　1914 年耶誕節，發生了不尋常的事。德國和英國開戰已將近五個月。雙方陣營每天有成千上萬名士兵送命或受傷。這些士兵疲累不堪又想念故國親人。雖然不得不盡責打贏戰爭，但他們寧願停下來不打了。這正是發生在耶誕節的事，至少是維持了一小段時間。部分士兵暫停射擊敵人的每日任務，就在戰場上進行了一場足球賽。時至今日，全球各地耶誕節時都會舉行足球友誼賽，紀念第一次世界大戰期間這個特殊的和平時刻。人們也可以到利物浦聖路加教堂參觀耶誕節休戰雕塑，那是一名德軍士兵和一名英國士兵於足球上方握手言歡。

解析 :

D 1. 此題語意為德英兩國戰爭已持續近 5 個月，表示動作持續一段時間，又發生在過去，故使用<u>過去完成式</u> (had + 過去分詞)，故本題選 (D) had been。

C 2. 依據文章語意推測，戰爭中非死即傷，所以選 (C) injured (*adj.*) 受傷的，(A) excited (*adj.*) 興奮的 (B) satisfied (*adj.*) 滿足的 (D) adopted (*adj.*) 領養的，皆不符語意。

A 3. 根據語意是停戰，stop + V-ing 表示停止做…動作，故本題選 (A)。

B 4. S shoot at + O ...，表示「射擊…」，故本題選 (B) at。

D 5. (A) stay up 熬夜 (B) back up 支持 (C) take effect 起作用 (D) take place 舉行

Part 2 *Internship Makes You Stronger*

中譯：

　　許多學生趁暑假出遊。但有些人申請實習，獲取珍貴的工作經驗和攢錢。事實上，許多企業也透過網路或校方，積極尋求暑假實習生。根據那些曾經當過實習生的人表示，這對你的未來職涯有三大好處。一是了解產業。身為實習生，你有更多機會得知組織運作。另一個優點是，增加你的優勢。做為特殊專業的實習生，具有良好人際關係，你往後找工作時，更容易被錄取。再來就是，你的學業條件會更好。許多學校知道實習的價值，會給予學分。所以，如果你下個暑假沒有計畫，何不試試去實習？

解析：

B 1. (A) as long as 只要… (B) as well as 和… (C) as soon as 一…就… (D) as far as... 達到…一樣遠。 此題語意為 「但有些人申請實習，獲取珍貴的工作經驗和攢錢。」，所以選 (B)。

C 2. (A) Speaking of 說到；講到… (B) Regardless of 儘管 (C) According to 根據 (D) Except for 除…外，根據語意選 (C)。

A 3. 此題 ... have more chance to know 之後要接一個名詞子句，語意為有更多機會了解組織的樣貌。原句為 "what is an organization like?"，放在 know 之後當受詞，所以這邊要改成間接問句，才是名詞子句，故本題選 (A) what an organization is like。

B 4. (A) costly (*adj.*) 貴重的 (B) likely (*adj.*) 可能的 (C) friendly (*adj.*) 友善的 (D) lovely (*adj.*) 可愛的

C 5. 前述當實習生有三個主要的好處，已經提了兩個，剩下最後一個，當表示有三個對象時用 One, another, the other... (一…，另一…，還有一…)，所以本題選 (C) The other。 ⇨ ➕ **文法加油站 2**

Unit 7

中譯：

　　雨林在維持全球氣候上扮演要角。不幸的是，人們每年在全球各地摧毀20萬平方公里的雨林。面積大約是臺灣的5.5倍。巴西和印尼的問題更為嚴重。事實上，這兩個國家似乎爭先恐後的想早些砍光他們的雨林。以前，巴西是明顯的贏家，以比印尼快很多的速度砍掉大片雨林。然而，印尼加速清除雨林，現在已經超越巴西。這項競賽的贏家是靠伐木出售賺大錢的企業主。輸家是誰？住在這個地球上的所有植物、動物和人類。

解析：

C 1.(A) criticize (*v.*) 批評 (B) ignore (*v.*) 忽視 (C) destroy (*v.*) 破壞 (D) signal (*v.*) 做手勢

A 2.根據上下文的文意，巴西和印尼情況最糟；事實上，這兩國好像在比賽似的，故選 (A) In fact。

D 3.分詞構句的省略用法，原句為：Brazil was the ..., and cut down... 省略連接詞 and，將 cut 改為分詞 cutting (因為是主動的動作)。

A 4.(A) effort (*n.*) 努力 (B) calendar (*n.*) 日曆 (C) career (*n.*) 職涯 (D) glance (*n.*) 一瞥

B 5.(A) threat (*n.*) 威脅 (B) profit (*n.*) 利益 (C) resource (*n.*) 資源 (D) habitat (*n.*) 棲息地

中譯 :

　　你喜歡看電影嗎？很多人都喜歡。那麼一些關於電影的事一定能引起你的興趣。電影剛發明時，是無聲的黑白片。許多默片會上字幕，提示觀眾和故事有關的訊息。此外，戲院還會聘請樂師在播映時演奏。樂曲類型取決於電影場景。悲劇或浪漫場景用節奏較緩慢的音樂，喜劇和動作場景則用較輕快活潑的音樂。隨著科技進步，有聲音的電影問世。觀眾不僅聽得到聲音，也聽得到演員講話。這些新電影因此被稱為「有聲片」。大家不敢置信。有些人甚至認為有聲片不是好點子。時間顯然已證明他們看法錯誤。這些了不起的改變讓電影更受歡迎。

解析 :

B 1. 原句為：When movies were first invented, they were in black...，將 when 引導的副詞子句改為分詞構句。因為是被動，所以只留下 Vpp (invented) 即可。
　　⇨ ➕ **文法加油站 1**

D 2. 此為 provide 的用法，provide sb. with sth. = provide sth. for sb.，故選 (D) with。

C 3. (A) result in 導致 (B) look into 調查 (C) depend on 視⋯而定 (D) search for 尋找，該句意為所播放的音樂類型視正在放映的場景而定，故選 (C)。

B 4. (A) recovery (*n.*) 復原 (B) technology (*n.*) 科技 (C) target (*n.*) 目標 (D) recipe (*n.*) 食譜

C 5. (A) Particularly (*adv.*) 尤其 (B) Globally (*adv.*) 全球地 (C) Obviously (*adv.*) 顯然 (D) Hardly (*adv.*) 幾乎不

Unit 8

Part 1 *Getting Married in a Unique Way*

中譯 :

結婚是人生重要大事。大部分新人想穿傳統禮服舉行教堂婚禮。然而,如今有愈來愈多的新人選擇辦一場非傳統婚禮。 有些點子是如此瘋狂以致於讓你瞠目結舌。例如,有新人以高空跳傘、潛行海底,萬聖節變裝、搭熱氣球等方式締結良緣。事實上,人們結婚的方式無奇不有。據報導有場婚禮在星巴克咖啡店舉行。更令人嘖嘖稱奇的是另一場在天體營海灘舉行的婚禮,賓客也全裸出席。誰知道呢?也許這篇文章會激發你的靈感,有天舉辦一場與眾不同的婚禮!

解析 :

C 1.(A) identity (*n.*) 身分 (B) background (*n.*) 背景 (C) ceremony (*n.*) 典禮 (D) captain (*n.*) 隊長;機長

B 2.此題為 so...that... 的用法,為表示結果的副詞子句,表示「如此⋯以致於⋯」。此句語意為「有些點子是如此瘋狂以致於讓你⋯」。

A 3. There be + N + V-ing (分詞片語修飾前面的名詞) ,因為主詞為動作的主動發生者,因此動詞為現在分詞 (V-ing)。

A 4.(A) take place 舉行 (B) take off 起飛 (C) take effect 起作用 (D) take cover 躲藏

C 5.形容詞子句修飾先行詞 beach,因 beach 是場所,又子句已完整 (不缺主詞),故選關係副詞 where。

中譯：

　　12 月 25 日是全球許多國家節慶日。然而，耶誕節的各項傳統絕對不限於 12 月 25 日。許多耶誕相關的活動發生在 1 月 5 日，這是耶誕期間的第 12 天，也是最後一天。除了裝飾耶誕樹和互贈禮物外，西方人還會做些什麼呢？例如在德國，小孩子習慣晚上上床睡覺前，在臥室門外留一隻鞋。早上，他們會發現鞋裡塞滿糖果。在法國，人們會分享一種叫做國王蛋糕的傳統糕點。國王蛋糕裡有一個小玩偶。誰吃到那塊裡面藏有小玩偶的蛋糕，就成為「國王」或「皇后」，可以戴上漂亮的紙皇冠。不用說也知道，每個小孩都想成為那個幸運兒。

解析：

C 1. (A) popular with 受喜愛或歡迎 (B) ashamed of 以…為恥 (C) associated with 和…有關 (D) capable of 有能力做…。　這裡原是形容詞子句 which are associated with...，但省略 which are，成為形容詞片語。

D 2. 此題語意為「除了裝飾聖誕樹和互贈禮物外，西方人還會做些什麼呢？」
(A) Because of 因為 (B) Out of 出於 (C) In spite of 儘管，因此選 (D) In addition to。

A 3. (A) for example 例如 (B) such as + N 例如 (C) as a result 因此 (D) above all 尤其。前一句問西方人還會做些什麼事來過耶誕節？此句便以德國為例，其後沒有加名詞，因此選 (A) for example。

B 4. 此句型為 S + find + O + Adj (OC)，表示「發現…」。full of = filled with 塞滿 / 擠滿 / 充滿，由於 find 後受詞須接形容詞，因此選 (B) full。

B 5. (A) vacancy (*n.*) 空缺；空房 (B) honor (*n.*) 榮譽 (C) appearance (*n.*) 外觀，外表 (D) weight (*n.*) 重量

Unit 9

中譯 :

是測試你物理知識的時候了！說到建造橋樑，你覺得用什麼材質可建造結構強固的建築物？石頭？答得好。金屬？更好。未烹調過的義大利麵條？棒透了！雖然聽來古怪，但許多大學工程科系都在辦比賽，要學生設計搭「義大利麵條橋」。一座全以未烹調過的義大利麵條和漿糊製作的小型橋樑。比賽規則各不相同，但有所大學要求，這座橋必須能架在 40 公分寬的間距上。能在橋樑中央承重力達 5 秒就是贏家。這種比賽是個獨特有趣的方法，可多面向測試學生的工程知識，例如壓力、角度、作用力等等。這是否讓你有興趣自己蓋座橋呢？

解析 :

A 1.(A) structure (*n.*) 建築物 ； 結構 (B) planet (*n.*) 行星 (C) ambition (*n.*) 抱負 (D) impression (*n.*) 印象

D 2.此句原為 ...contests are held and in the contests students must design...，將 and 後的子句改為關係子句，關係代名詞代替 the contests，此時介係詞 in 仍保留，所以選 (D) in which。

A 3.此句原為 a little bridge which is made entirely of... ， 當關係代名詞為子句的主詞時，可將關係子句簡化成分詞片語，即可省略 which is。

B 4. that 引導關係子句 (即形容詞子句) 修飾先行詞 bridge，that 是子句裡的主詞，故不可省略，亦可用 which。

C 5.(A) chemical (*adj.*) 化學的 (B) following (*adj.*) 下列的 (C) unique (*adj.*) 獨特的 (D) royal (*adj.*) 皇家的

中譯：

　　現代生活型態是怎樣的呢?長時間工作和讀書是現代社會日常生活的一部分。結果導致，人們經常忙到無法獲得充足睡眠。然而，現在長期缺乏睡眠被認為是重大健康風險的因素。50年前，醫生才理解到抽菸對人體的傷害，開始建議戒菸。研究人員相信，說到睡眠，我們現在處於差不多的境況。研究顯示，連短期的睡眠不足都能使血壓飆高，並影響血糖。肥胖和情緒問題也和睡得太少有關。當然，我們需要的睡眠量人人不同，但一般而言，每晚少於六小時被認為很不健康。所以，為了健康的緣故，就算忙的不得了，也最好獲得充足睡眠。

解析：

B　1. be recognized as 表示「被認為是…」，所以選 (B) as。

A　2. 此句為意志動詞 recommend 的用法，表示「建議…」，that 後常省略助動詞 should，因此其後接原形動詞，故選 (A) quit。⇨ ➕ **文法加油站** 1

D　3. (A) Politician (*n.*) 政客 (B) Customer (*n.*) 顧客 (C) Applicant (*n.*) 申請者 (D) Researcher (*n.*) 研究者

A　4. (A) raise (*v.*) 提高 (B) appeal (*v.*) 吸引 (C) debate (*v.*) 爭論 (D) permit (*v.*) 允許

D　5. 前一句是在述說睡眠的需求量因人而異，後面則說少於六小時是具傷害性的，而 (D) generally speaking 意思是「一般而言」，作為句中的轉折語合乎語意。其餘選項均不符合語意，(A) no longer 不再 (B) on the contrary 相反地 (C) at once 立刻。

Part 1 *Internet Security*

中譯：

　　在資訊時代，我們的工作和私生活都愈發仰賴網際網路。這樣一來，資訊安全就是一大隱憂。有許多人的身份遭駭客竊取後生活變調的驚悚報導。不講也知道，有必要設定難破解的密碼。不幸的是，特殊電腦病毒能輕易竊取你所有的密碼。這是為什麼一些網路服務，像是 Google 和 Facebook 建議使用兩步驟密碼。步驟 1 以正常方式輸入你的密碼。步驟 2，輸入以簡訊傳到你手機的數字碼。這讓駭客較難入侵你的線上帳戶。畢竟再怎麼小心謹慎也不為過。

解析：

B 1. (A) device (*n.*) 裝置 (B) security (*n.*) 安全 (C) tendency (*n.*) 趨勢 (D) faith (*n.*) 信心

D 2. 關係代名詞引導形容詞子句修飾先行詞 people，因其後接名詞 identity，所以用所有格 whose。

A 3. 此題是 it 為虛主詞的用法，It + be + Adj + to V，真正的主詞，是後面的 to have a very strong password。 ⇨ ➕ **文法加油站 2**

C 4. 此句型表示「這是為什麼一些網路服務…」，故選 (C) why，其句型為 That is why / what / when / how / where + S + V。

A 5. (A) involve (*v.*) 包含 (B) absorb (*v.*) 吸收 (C) appreciate (*v.*) 欣賞 (D) construct (*v.*) 建造

中譯：

　　如我們所知，閱讀在我們的生活裡扮演要角。能讓我們的生活更豐富。不講也知道，這種好習慣必須從小培養，因為閱讀能力是兒童教育的重要關鍵之一。有些小孩天生會讀書，就像鴨子善泳一般。美國密西根州一位理髮師想出一個新奇好點子，鼓勵當地小學生多唸書。理髮時大聲朗讀的小孩能獲得 2 塊美金的優惠。這對理髮師、父母和小孩來說都是好事。隨著消息傳開來，街坊鄰居都來捐書。自從開始推展這個了不起的計畫以來，有數不清的孩子加入。那些幸運兒不僅理髮較省錢，也獲得一項人生珍寶——閱讀。

解析：

A 1.(A) develop (*v.*) 培養，發展 (B) debate (*v.*) 爭論 (C) decline (*v.*) 衰退 (D) declare (*v.*) 使沮喪

D 2.(A) get rid of 擺脫；去除 (B) cut down on 減少⋯的量 (C) run out of 用完 (D) come up with 想出

C 3.此句原為 Kids who read out loud while they were having their hair cut... ，表示「當孩子們在理髮時出聲讀書⋯」，將 while 引導的副詞子句改為分詞構句，也就是省略 they were，變成 while + V-ing，其餘選項皆不符合語意。

A 4.(A) As 隨著 (B) Though 雖然 (C) Even if 即使 (D) Because of 因為 。選項 (D) 在語意上雖可接受，但其後須接子句，而非受詞，故不選 (D) Because of。

B 5. Since + S + V-ed, S + have / has + Vpp。此為現在完成式的用法。又因 there 之後所接的名詞為複數 (countless kids)，故選 (B) have been。

Part 1 *The Midas Touch*

中譯：

　　英文裡，「點金術」指的是有賺錢天賦的人。這種說法來自希臘神話，神賜予一個名叫麥達斯的國王一種點石成金的能力。有了這本事，他能將任何東西變成黃金，只要碰一下就行。剛開始，這個國王很開心，貪心的將許多東西變做黃金。他樂不可支，跑去抱女兒。然而，他一碰到她，她就變成金像。他嚇壞了，嘗試所有可能的辦法要把女兒變回來。但無論如何努力都沒法讓她復活。直至此時，他才了解這項能力其實是個詛咒。雖然成為天下首富，他卻是全世界最不快樂的人。

解析：

A 1. 此句原為 ...about a king <u>who was</u> named Midas... 將畫線部分的形容詞子句省略 who was，簡化成分詞片語 named...。

D 2. 此句語意為「有了這本事，他能將…」，因此選 (D) with 有，其餘選項不符語意。

B 3. (A) confused (*adj.*) 感到困惑的 (B) delighted (*adj.*) 欣喜的 (C) annoyed (*adj.*) 氣惱的 (D) frustrated (*adj.*) 感到挫折的

D 4. (A) even though 即便 (B) as if 就好像 (C) in spite of 儘管。此句語意為「他一碰到她，她就變成金像」，因此選 (D) as soon as 一…就…，as soon as 引導副詞子句，用以連接幾乎同時發生的動作。⇨ ➕ **文法加油站** 1

C 5. No matter what 無論什麼 (B) No matter when 無論何時 (D) No matter who 無論誰；此句語意為「無論如何努力都沒法讓她復活。」，因此選 (C) No matter how 無論如何，其餘選項皆不符合語意。

Part 2 *The Urban Legend*

中譯：

聽說過「都市傳說」嗎？都市傳說是些稀奇古怪、令人意外或感到驚異的網路謠言。被稱做網路謠言的原因在於，這些眾所周知的故事通常是無中生有或僅有部分為真。以下是都市傳說的範例。據說創辦迪士尼公司的華特・迪士尼計畫死後冷凍大腦，希望科學家有一天能讓他起死回生。這是個典型的都市傳說，即使所有證據都證明這是無稽之談，但還是有人信以為真。類似故事讀起來挺有趣的，但在分享給朋友之前，你最好弄清楚它們不是都市傳說。也就是別讓自己難堪，否則你可能變成朋友圈裡的笑柄。

解析：

B 1. (A) burst out 突然 (接 V-ing) (B) made up 編造 (C) set out 出發 (D) used up 用完，用光

A 2. 此句型為 It is said that S + V，表示「據說；人們說」。 ⇨ ➕ **文法加油站 1**

C 3. (A) peace (*n.*) 和平 (B) harvest (*n.*) 收穫 (C) evidence (*n.*) 證據 (D) challenge (*n.*) 挑戰

B 4. (A) lead to 導致；通往 (B) make sure 確定 (C) major in 主修 (D) dress up 盛裝

D 5. avoid 表示「避免」，其後可加 V-ing 或名詞，故選 (D) embarrassing。

Unit 12

Part 1 *It's Not All About Making Money*

中譯：

　　有時，我喜歡到市立動物園玩。我們有個很棒的動物園，裡面住了來自全球各地的動物，職員把牠們照顧得很好。觀賞這些動物讓我想到我們為什麼要有動物園。理由之一是娛樂大眾以營利。訪客來看動物餵食、玩耍和閒逛。除非到非洲去，否則動物園也許是你能看到活生生的獅子或長頸鹿的唯一機會。但這其實不全然為了賺錢。動物園有助於保護瀕危物種。它們也教育和促使人類更在乎且願意為未來世代的人們看顧地球。所以，下次你去動物園時，多想想你能為動物做些什麼。

解析：

A 1.(A) creature (*n.*) 生物 (B) career (*n.*) 生涯 (C) decoration (*n.*) 裝飾 (品) (D) degree (*n.*) 度；學位

D 2.若主詞為動作的話，須將動詞改為動名詞，因此選 (D) Looking。

B 3.(A) because 因為 (B) unless 除非 (C) though 雖然 (D) meanwhile 同時；此句語意為「除非到非洲去，否則動物園也許是你能看到活生生的獅子或長頸鹿的唯一機會。」，因此選 (B) unless 除非，其餘選項皆不符合語意。

A 4. help + to V，to 可以省略，故此題選 (A) protect。

D 5.(A) symbol (*n.*) 象徵 (B) description (*n.*) 描述 (C) journey (*n.*) 旅行 (D) generation (*n.*) 世代

中譯：

　　研究顯示，每天笑開懷有助維持體態和健康。笑也有助病患更快康復。在「倫敦愛笑俱樂部」這裡，我們當然相信此事不假。笑也是一種心理運動，有助你對人生抱持愉悅、無壓力和積極正面的態度。助益最大的是笑得長久且用力，但這靠一己之力不易達到。這是為什麼我們每日有大型聚會，在經驗老道的「愛笑領導人」引導下練習開懷大笑。來加入我們的陣容！第一堂課完全免費。如果你害羞，帶個伴來！上網到 *londonlaughterclub.net* 查詢。我們期待你大駕光臨。千萬抓住這個可以變得更健康快樂的難得機會。直到你來你才會知道有何好事發生。

解析：

A 1.(A) mental (*adj.*) 心理的 (B) upset (*adj.*) 生氣的；不舒服的 (C) digital (*adj.*) 數位的 (D) curious (*adj.*) 好奇的

D 2.(A) opportunity (*n.*) 機會 (B) leisure (*n.*) 閒暇時間 (C) flood (*n.*) 水災 (D) advantage (*n.*) 好處

B 3. with + O + OC (Adj / V-ing / Vpp) 表附帶狀況。該句語意為「我們每日有大型聚會，在經驗老道的「愛笑領導人」引導下…」(引導是<u>主動動作</u>，不是被指導)。所以這裡受詞補語 (OC) 選擇 (B) guiding (主動)。

C 4.此句語意為「如果你害羞，帶個伴來！」為祈使句，故選原形動詞 (C) come。

D 5.(A) rely on 依賴 (B) carry out 實施；實行 (C) put up with 忍受 (D) look forward to 期待

20分鐘稱霸統測
英文字彙

陳曉菁／編著

- 篩選近年統測常考的單字與近義詞組，補充豐富字詞用法、同義字與通用搭配。
- 20回練習題符合近年統測出題趨勢，取材多元，可培養生活知識素養。
- 解析夾冊加碼「單字隨身GO」單元，背單字、複習帶這本就夠！

20分鐘稱霸統測 英文閱讀測驗

吳昱樺／編著

- 坊間唯一主打「素養導向」的閱讀測驗參考書，邏輯思考單元、圖表情境題一應俱全。精心設計14回主題式閱測單元，程度分級設計、難度由淺入深。隨書附贈解析本，讀者可輕鬆自學。

- 解題攻略篇包含7大閱讀技巧，提升學生英文閱讀能力，並幫助學生快速掌握文章內容。實戰測驗篇精選42篇符合108新課綱議題之文章。

- Pre-reading Questions：引導式問題單元，幫助學生在進入文章前，對該主題有初步概念。

- Target Vocabulary：圖像式單字學習，以視覺記憶加深單字印象。

- After You Read：剖析文章結構，幫助學生理解文意、抓住文章重點。

- Practice：透過練習檢視字彙學習成效，加強字彙實力以累積閱讀能力。

英文科
歷屆統測試題

黃宏祿、楊凱全／編著

本書特色：

一、彙集各學年度四技二專統一入學測驗之
英文科試題，年代由近至遠排列，讀者
可藉此馬上熟悉最新命題趨勢，並且深
入掌握歷屆命題重點，未來方向不再迷惘。

二、每一學年試題後皆附完整解答及詳細解析，包括題型分析、命題重點、解
題技巧、題目翻譯與字彙補充，讓讀者由此五方面深入試題核心，在考場
上輕鬆獲得高分。